THE ULTIMATE GUIDE TO
DEVELOPING LEADERS

Introducing John Maxwell Publishing

In 1976, after speaking to a group of leaders at a Fourth of July event, Dr. John C. Maxwell left the stage with an unquestionable sense of calling in his heart: to add value to leaders who would multiply value to others. That sense of purpose drove Dr. Maxwell to begin his decades-long dedication to the study and training of leadership and resulted in the global transformation movement he oversees today.

The outflow of that legacy is best represented by Dr. Maxwell's writing. With over one hundred books to his credit, Dr. Maxwell's output has changed millions of lives across the globe. In almost any room where he speaks, he is preceded by at least one book that has impacted and shaped the life of a leader, confirming his belief that writing allows him to touch a leader he might otherwise never meet in-person.

It is in keeping with Dr. Maxwell's calling and belief about the power of words to impact leaders that HarperCollins Publishers and the John Maxwell Company have created the John Maxwell Publishing imprint, a new leadership-focused division of HarperCollins Publishers that seeks to extend and expand Dr. Maxwell's legacy.

The mission of John Maxwell Publishing is to discover and publish books that identify with John Maxwell's personal values and philosophy of leadership. The authors will be men and women of integrity in their personal, business, and spiritual lives, who have demonstrated a desire to add value to leaders who multiply that value to people, whether through their teaching, writing, or business acumen.

As Dr. Maxwell himself has said, "One is too small a number to achieve greatness." Through this imprint, Dr. Maxwell's calling to add value to leaders who multiply value to others will not only continue but strengthen. These authors will add to and expand on his vision of transformation around the world.

THE ULTIMATE GUIDE TO
DEVELOPING
LEADERS

INVEST *in* PEOPLE
LIKE YOUR FUTURE
DEPENDS *on* IT

JOHN C.
MAXWELL

HARPERCOLLINS
LEADERSHIP

AN IMPRINT OF HARPERCOLLINS

Published by HarperCollins Leadership, an imprint of HarperCollins Focus LLC.

Published in association with Yates & Yates, www.yates2.com.

Any internet addresses, phone numbers, or company or product information printed in this book are offered as a resource and are not intended in any way to be or to imply an endorsement by HarperCollins Leadership, nor does HarperCollins Leadership vouch for the existence, content, or services of these sites, phone numbers, companies, or products beyond the life of this book.

Scripture quotations marked ASV are from the Authorized Standard Version. Public domain.

Scripture quotations marked MSG are taken from THE MESSAGE, copyright © 1993, 2002, 2018 by Eugene H. Peterson. Used by permission of NavPress. All rights reserved. Represented by Tyndale House Publishers, Inc.

Scripture quotations marked NIV are taken from the Holy Bible, New International Version®, NIV®. Copyright © 1973, 1978, 1984, 2011 by Biblica, Inc.™ Used by permission of Zondervan. All rights reserved worldwide. www.zondervan.com. The "NIV" and "New International Version" are trademarks registered in the United States Patent and Trademark Office by Biblica, Inc.™

Scripture quotations marked NKJV are taken from the New King James Version®. Copyright © 1982 by Thomas Nelson. Used by permission. All rights reserved.

Derived from material previously published in The Leader's Greatest Return: Attracting, Developing, and Multiplying Leaders

ISBN 978-1-4002-4621-2 (HC)
ISBN 978-1-4002-4694-6 (eBook)
ISBN 978-1-4002-4722-6 (IE)

Library of Congress Control Number

Printed in the United States of America
23 24 25 26 27 LBC 5 4 3 2 1

CONTENTS

ACKNOWLEDGMENT

I want to say thank you to Charlie Wetzel and the rest of the team who assisted me with the formation and publication of this book. And to the people in my organizations who support it. You all add incredible value to me, which allows me to add value to others. Together, we're making a difference!

ONE

UNDERSTAND THAT DEVELOPING LEADERS IS THE ANSWER

When conducting leadership conferences, I am asked a lot of questions about how to solve problems and overcome challenges. Most often, people want to know how to improve and grow an organization. My answer is straightforward: Develop leaders. If you grow a leader, you can grow the organization. If you don't, you can't. A company cannot grow throughout until its leaders grow within.

I am often amazed at the amount of money and energy organizations spend on activities that will *not* produce growth. They pour money into marketing, yet they don't train their employees in how to treat their customers. You can say customers are your priority, but they know the difference between good service and hollow promises. Slick advertising and catchy slogans will never overcome incompetent leadership.

Or they reorganize, hoping that shuffling people around will produce growth. That doesn't work. You can move around the crew of the *Titanic*, but the ship is still going to sink!

Or they rewrite their mission statement. Or rename their departments. Or cut costs. Or spend more. None of those activities will produce the results that developing leaders will. The strength of any organization is a direct result of the strength of its leaders. Weak leaders equal weak organizations. Strong leaders equal strong organizations. Leadership makes the determination.

If you lead a team or organization, no matter whether your goal is to grow your company, increase sales, develop a new product, establish a new location, launch a new initiative, create a new team, or enter a new industry, your success will be determined by the number of leaders you have and their ability to lead.

THE UNBELIEVABLE RETURN OF DEVELOPING LEADERS

For any team, small business, large corporation, nonprofit organization, or government entity, the key to accomplishing today's goals and achieving tomorrow's dreams is leadership. And the surefire way to improve the leadership of your organization or team is to develop leaders yourself.

There are innumerable benefits that come from having developed leaders working with you. Here are ten.

1. ORGANIZATIONS WITH DEVELOPED LEADERS OUTPERFORM THE COMPETITION

The better the leaders in an organization, the more successful it can become. A recent report published by human resources consulting firm Development Dimensions International stated:

Organizations with the highest quality leaders were 13 times more likely to outperform their competition in key bottom-line metrics such as financial performance, quality of products and services, employee engagement, and customer satisfaction. Specifically, when leaders reported their organization's current leadership quality as poor, only 6 percent of them were in organizations that outperformed their competition. Compare that with those who rated their organization's leadership quality as excellent—78 percent were in organizations that outperformed their competition in bottom-line metrics.[1]

Wouldn't you like your organization or team to be thirteen times more likely to outperform your competition? The surefire way to get high-quality leaders is to develop them.

2. Developed Leaders Multiply Your Resources

When people become successful, they always eventually hit a wall where they realize that their resources are more limited than their vision. There's so much we all want to do, yet we get frustrated by our limitations. What's the solution to this dilemma? Developing leaders. Good leaders increase resources in a way that nothing else does. Look at how they do this:

- **Time:** The more and better leaders you team up with, the more time you gain back because you can delegate authority and tasks to others you know will follow through with excellence.
- **Thinking:** As the leaders on your team develop, they become wiser and more valuable as advisers. When a team of good thinkers works together, good thoughts become great thoughts.
- **Production:** Gathering together a team of developed leaders is like giving yourself the ability to be in many places at once. No

longer does everything in your world need to be touched by you to become productive. Others can carry the ball, develop teams, and lead.

- **People:** As leaders are developed, they attract other like-minded people. The more powerful the team you build, the more others want to be part of it. Your leaders can recruit for you and further develop the organization.
- **Loyalty:** When you develop people, their lives improve. As a result, they are usually very grateful. As an added bonus, they also often develop personal loyalty. That makes your life that much sweeter.

The leaders who work with me have made it possible for my organizations to accomplish so much more than I could have on my own. There's really no comparison. I can only do so much personally. But there's no limit to what all these leaders can do.

3. DEVELOPED LEADERS HELP YOU CARRY YOUR LEADERSHIP LOAD

Leadership can be difficult. Most leaders carry heavy loads and feel that there are too few hours in a day. If you're a lone leader, you carry all that weight; but when you have other leaders working with you, that weight can be shared. You simply need to be willing to give some of it to them. If you feel that your team, department, shift, or organization doesn't run well when you're not there, either you haven't developed leaders to help you, or you haven't been willing to let go of responsibilities.

4. DEVELOPED LEADERS HELP YOU CREATE MOMENTUM

The Law of the Big Mo in *The 21 Irrefutable Laws of Leadership* says momentum is a leader's best friend.[2] Why is that? Because momentum makes large problems small, average people excellent, and positive change possible.

I like what speaker and consultant Michael McQueen said about momentum:

> Momentum truly gives you an unfair advantage when it's working on your side. . . .
>
> When you've got momentum on your side, you don't need to develop clever strategies for recruiting staff or persuading customers—both will be attracted to you because you are going somewhere and they want to be a part of it.
>
> Just as love covers a multitude of sins in the personal realm, momentum covers a multitude of sins in the professional arena.
>
> Having momentum working for you makes you appear more talented and clever than you really are. When momentum is on your side, you get disproportionately more than you deserve through the power of leverage. Conversely, when momentum is working against you, it's easy to appear ill-fated and incompetent—when neither may actually be the case.[3]

What is the best way to create momentum? Harness the positive power of good leadership. Leaders are all about forward movement. They love progress more than anything else. Trying to create momentum on your own is like trying to push a four-thousand-pound vehicle by yourself. Can you do it? Maybe on a flat surface. But wouldn't it be easier if a dozen people with similar strength helped you? Not only could a group of you push it; you could probably get it moving pretty fast. And you could even push it uphill if you had to—especially if you were allowed to develop the momentum of a running start. A group of developed leaders gives a similar advantage to your organization.

5. DEVELOPED LEADERS EXPAND YOUR INFLUENCE

Years ago, when I first started receiving invitations to speak to groups, I made a decision. If I had a choice, I would always choose to speak to leaders. Why? Because I knew that when I spoke to a group of followers, I could help them. But when I spoke to a group of leaders, I could help not only them, but all the people they help. That's why I'd rather teach a hundred leaders instead of a thousand followers. When I influence leaders, I influence all the people they influence.

About a decade ago, the presidents of several nations began contacting me to ask if my organizations would come to their countries to teach values. I've gladly made trips to Guatemala, Paraguay, Costa Rica, the Dominican Republic, Papua New Guinea, Panama, and Brazil to speak to individual heads of state. By talking with one person, I was pursuing the opportunity to influence the millions of people they influenced.

When you develop leaders and they work with you, their influence joins yours. For every single leader you influence, your impact extends to all the people they influence. The greater the talent and influence of that leader, the greater it expands your reach.

6. DEVELOPED LEADERS KEEP YOU ON YOUR TOES

Nothing keeps a leader on his or her toes better than leading a group of leaders who are being developed. When the team you lead is growing, you have to keep growing to keep leading them well. In his book *Up Your Business! 7 Steps to Fix, Build, or Stretch Your Organization*, my friend Dave Anderson wrote:

> The primary reason so few leaders or organizations ever become great is because they get good and they stop. They stop growing, learning,

risking, and changing. They use their track record or prior successes as evidence they've arrived. Believing their own headlines, the leaders in these successful organizations are ready to write it down, build the manual, and document the formula. This mentality shifts their business from a growth to maintenance mind-set and trades in innovation for optimization.[4]

It's dangerous to think you've arrived as a leader. As someone once quipped, today's peacocks are tomorrow's feather dusters. If you want to keep leading, you need to keep growing, and few things stretch a leader like developing leaders who are committed to growing.

> Today's peacocks are tomorrow's feather dusters.

7. Developed Leaders Ensure a Better Future for Your Organization

G. Alan Bernard, president of manufacturing company Mid-Park, Inc., said, "A good leader will always have those around him who are better at particular tasks than he is. This is the hallmark of leadership. Never be afraid to hire or manage people who are better at certain jobs than you are. They can only make your organization stronger."[5] I would add to that, never be afraid to develop people who are better than you are.

My organizations are filled with developed leaders who do particular tasks better than I do. I know that the future of my organization is bright because the leaders who will carry on after I am no longer able to lead. How about yours? If you got sick, left your organization, or retired, what kind of a future would your organization have? If you have developed strong and capable leaders, and you have trained them to develop more, the future will be bright.

YOU CAN DEVELOP LEADERS

If you are a leader—at any level or in any capacity—your organization will benefit when you start developing leaders. The good news is that leaders can be developed. And here's more good news: even if you've never trained, coached, or developed another person before, you can learn to do it now. And I want to help you.

It's taken me decades to learn what I know about developing leaders. I've had my failures, as well as my successes. I want you to benefit from those so that you can be successful right away. As you take this leadership journey, there are three things you need to prepare yourself for:

8. Developing Leaders Is Difficult

If you've ever led people in any capacity, I think you'll agree that leadership is hard work. There are no two consecutive easy days in the life of leaders. If today is easy, you know tomorrow probably won't be. But everything worthwhile is uphill. If the purpose of life was ease and comfort, no sensible person would ever take on the demands of leadership.

Developing leaders is even harder. It's like herding cats. That is why so many leaders content themselves with attracting and leading followers instead of seeking out and developing leaders. Followers usually follow. Leaders, not so much.

> "I don't promise you it will be easy. I do promise you it will be worthwhile."
>
> —ART WILLIAMS

However, the work of investing your life in developing other leaders has a high return. As my friend Art Williams is apt to say, "I don't promise you it will be easy. I do promise you it will be worthwhile."[6] Get ready to do the work.

9. DEVELOPING LEADERS TAKES TIME

Gayle Beebe, the president of Westmont College, has studied leadership development extensively. In *The Shaping of an Effective Leader*, he wrote:

> Our understanding of leadership does not come to us all at once. It takes time. In our instant-oriented culture we often want to short-circuit the thinking, reflecting and acting that mark our progressive development as leaders. Understanding how leaders develop and why they matter requires discernment, wisdom and insight.[7]

It also requires time. If developing ourselves as leaders is a long, ongoing process, then we should also expect the development of others in leadership to be the same.

Recently, I visited a Napa Valley vineyard with friends, and the vineyard's third-generation owner pointed out a stone wall. He explained that his grandfather, the founder, had started building the wall. Later, the founder's son had added to it, as had his son, the current owner. Listening to him speak and show us the different sections of the wall, I could sense his pride and the respect for his father and grandfather. There was a sense of tradition and a shared vision that had crossed the generations. There was a strong sense of legacy, which is something that cannot be rushed.

If you desire to do something worthwhile, you have to let go of a microwave mind-set for developing leaders. The process can't be done instantly. It's slow, like a Crock-Pot. Anything worthwhile takes time. You must give up looking to cross a finish line and instead find your own internal fulfillment line. That's something you can cross every day when you embrace the process of developing leaders.

---

10. DEVELOPING LEADERS PUT YOUR DREAMS WITHIN REACH

People too often overvalue their dream and undervalue their team. They think, *If I believe it, I can achieve it.* But that's simply not true. Belief alone is not enough to achieve anything. It takes more than that. Your team will determine the reality of your dream. A big dream with a bad team is a nightmare.

> If you desire to fulfill a bold vision or do something great, you have to let go of a microwave mind-set for leadership.

One of my favorite quotes is by nineteenth-century steel magnate and philanthropist Andrew Carnegie. He said, "I think a fit epitaph for me would be, 'Here lies a man who knew how to get around men much cleverer than himself.'"[8] The only surefire way to achieve something like that is to develop more leaders so that they reach their potential, and that's not something any leader can afford to delegate or abdicate. It takes a leader to show and grow another leader.

My desire in this book is to take you through the entire process, step by step, for developing leaders. If you desire to improve your team and achieve your dreams, you will need to take each of the following steps:

1. Commit to Becoming a Developer of People
2. Get to Know Your Team Members
3. Equip Team Members to Excel at Their Jobs
4. Identify Your Potential Leaders
5. Invite People with Potential to the Leadership Table
6. Know the Goal of Developing Your Leaders
7. Empower New Leaders to Lead
8. Harness Your Leaders' Natural Motivation
9. Challenge Your Leaders to Work as a Team

10. Choose Who to Develop Further
11. Mentor Your Best Leaders One-on-One
12. Teach Your Leaders to Develop Other Leaders

My friend Zig Ziglar used to say, "Success is the maximum utilization of the ability that you have."[9] I love that definition, and I believe it applies to an individual. But for a leader, success requires something more. Success for leaders can be defined as the maximum utilization of the abilities of those working *with* them. There's only one way for a leader to help people maximize their abilities and reach their potential, and that's to help them develop as leaders. If, like me, you understand that is the answer, then let's get started.

> People too often overvalue their dream and undervalue their team. . . . A big dream with a bad team is a nightmare.

ACTION STEPS

1. List the long-term goals of your team or organization. You may also want to write out the big-picture vision the organization desires to achieve.

   _____

2. For each goal, write what efforts or initiatives have been implemented to try to achieve them. Then give a grade from A to F for the results of each.

   _____

3. What emphasis is currently being placed on developing leaders to achieve those goals and realize that vision?

   _____

4. Analyze where developed leaders could potentially achieve goals, how they could create progress, and what the outcome could be.

   _____

TWO

COMMIT TO BECOMING A DEVELOPER OF PEOPLE

We cannot reach our potential without the help of others. No person can. While self-evaluation is valuable, the perspective and assistance of people who are ahead of us in life and career are essential to our success. We all have blind spots where we lack self-awareness, and only another person can help us by providing another perspective. As a leader on your team or in your organization, you can help others go farther, move faster, and be more successful than they could ever be traveling on their own. You can do that by developing them.

What do I mean by becoming a developer of people? Developing people means adding value to them in any way you can. It means giving people time, attention, advice, and encouragement when they need it. It means making an investment in them without expecting anything specific from them in return. It means giving them a leg up to make them more successful.

Some people call this process coaching. Others call it mentoring. Some people ask if there is a difference. Here is how I see the two:

Coaching	Mentoring
Skill centered	Life centered
Formal setting	Informal setting
More structured	Less structured
Directive	Advisory
Short-term	Long-term
Narrow in scope	Broader in scope
Drives the agenda	Receives the agenda
Positional	Relational
Skill awareness	Self-awareness
Trains	Develops
Do something	Be something
Transactional	Transformational

Which should you focus on when beginning to develop people? That depends on what the person needs and what you have to offer. My interaction with particular people I'm developing is tailored to the them individually. But my goal is always the same: to help them go to the next level personally and professionally. I work to pour into them, challenge them, encourage them, and help them become their best. You must develop the person before you begin developing the leader.

GRATITUDE FOR THE LEADERS WHO INVESTED IN ME

Being developed has made a huge difference in my life. So has becoming a developer of people. For the leader, nothing is more fulfilling than developing other leaders. Not only is it personally rewarding, but it gives the biggest bang for the buck when it comes to personal investment and organizational success. Why? Because every person you develop is in a better position to positively impact other people. That's why my purpose is to add value to leaders who multiply value to others.

> You must develop the person before you begin developing the leader.

Peter Drucker is the person who clarified this in my mind. Back in the eighties, a small group of leaders and I spent several days at a retreat with him. On our last day together, he looked at the dozen of us in the room and said, "Everything I have said to you up to this point is not as important as what I am about to share with you now. Who are you going to develop?" He spent the next couple of hours talking to us about our responsibility as leaders to develop other leaders. It marked my life.

One of the people I admire most is John Wooden, the longtime coach of the UCLA Bruins basketball team. He was a coach, mentor, and developer of people, investing in his players in every way he could. In his book *A Game Plan for Life,* he wrote:

> I think if you truly understand the meaning of mentoring, you understand it is as important as parenting; in fact, it is just like parenting. As my father often said, "There is nothing you know that you haven't learned from someone else." Everything in the world has been passed down. Every piece of knowledge is something that has already been shared by someone else. If you understand it as I do, mentoring becomes your true legacy. It is the greatest inheritance you can give to others. It is why you get up every day—to teach and be taught.[1]

When I read those words, I'm stirred to think about all the people who have invested in me, who have given freely for my benefit. Whatever I can do today, whatever I can give, was made possible because I am standing on the shoulders of others. I'm humbled and grateful that leaders were willing to make deposits in my life, inspiring vision in me and teaching me life-changing principles. Here are some of the leaders who invested in me, along with the greatest lessons they taught me:

Dad (Melvin Maxwell)—*Having a great attitude is a choice.* He taught me that attitude is the difference maker.

Elmer Towns—*There is power in proximity.* He taught me to get close to the people who can make you better.

Lon Woodrum—*Go to places that inspire you.* He gave me the idea of visiting presidential libraries, and I've been to all of them.

Bob Kline—*Be the first to see potential in others.* He saw the potential in me when I was twenty-five, and I moved forward with greater confidence.

Les Parrott—*Expand your influence beyond your personal touch.* He encouraged me to start writing books.

Tom Phillippe—*Become your mentee's champion.* He was more than a mentor; he was a sponsor who put his reputation on the line for me so I could take risks and live outside the box.

Orval Butcher—*Carry the baton with excellence.* He asked me to be his successor and handed the leadership baton to me for the organization he founded and led for thirty-one years. I worked to carry it with excellence for fourteen years and then handed it off to the next leader.

J. Oswald Sanders—*Everything rises and falls on leadership.* He mentored me from a distance through his book *Spiritual Leadership*, which lit my fire to lead; I was able to meet him twenty years later to express my gratitude.

Fred Smith—*The gift is greater than the person.* He taught me that I should be grateful for the amazing gifts God gave me, but to remember that I am flawed, not amazing; that awareness grounded me.

Larry Maxwell (my brother)—*Develop different streams of income.* A talented businessman, he instructed me to create passive income that would work for me when I wasn't working.

Bill Bright—*Have a vision for the world.* He wanted to change the world, and every time I was with him, he expanded my vision and purpose.

Zig Ziglar—*Help others get what they want, and they will help you get what you want.* His statement prompted me to change the way I saw and practiced leadership, and I loved him for it.

Sealy Yates—*Take your message to the business world.* He encouraged me to include the business market when I wrote my books, and thirty-five million book sales later, we're still helping people.

Les Stobbe—*Will the reader turn the page?* Les coached me in how to write and make my message more compelling.

John Wooden—*Make every day your masterpiece.* He modeled his philosophy and was my greatest mentor; my book *Today Matters* was inspired by him.

I could continue this list, but I don't want to wear you out! My life has been shaped by leaders who coached, mentored, and developed me. I live on higher ground thanks to the people who have raised me up.

WHY SOME LEADERS DON'T EMPOWER OTHERS

I believe leaders know intuitively that they should be developing people. We know it's a great way to add value to others, improve their lives, and make our organizations more successful. However, too many leaders neglect the process. Why? Here are five reasons:

1. Lack of Awareness

Some leaders simply don't realize the importance of developing people, empowering them, and helping them to become leaders. If you have neglected to develop people in the past, I hope you now understand its importance and its power. And I hope you will commit to changing the way you lead. If you make the effort to develop people and empower them to lead, you will transform your leaders and your organization.

2. Lack of Time

Many leaders feel so much pressure to get tasks done that they never take a step back from *doing*, to see where they could be *developing* people and *releasing* them to take on greater roles. They miss the fact that people work harder and with more creativity when they've been developed and empowered to take ownership of an area. The tyranny of the urgent keeps many leaders shortsighted, where they are continually running to keep up instead of being intentional to work ahead.

3. Inability to Find Someone to Develop

Some leaders have difficulty finding people to develop. The have a hard time seeing potential in others. Or because they've never developed anyone before, they're not sure what to look for. If that describes you, don't worry. In the next three chapters, I'll walk you through the process of getting to know your team members, training them in the basics of their jobs, and observing them to identify potential leaders. From there, I'll show you how to take people through the further stages of development.

---

4. Lack of Belief in Others

Some leaders have a difficult time believing in people and placing their confidence in them. They fear they will be wasting their time when investing in others. Either they believe they won't get a positive return on their time, or they think others won't be capable of doing a job as well as they can. Both of those beliefs might be true. But those are not good reasons for not developing others. The reality is that you can't get much done if you always have to do everything yourself, or if you must personally direct every action you want others to take.

If your hesitance to develop people is a result of this kind of thinking, you may need to practice the 80 percent rule, which is what I do. If you can develop someone to do a task 80 percent as well as you do it, then delegate it. But you won't find that out until you develop others and begin to empower them. You have to give up being a perfectionist if you want to become a developer of people.

5. Reluctance Due to Past Failures

Seeing people rise to their potential is one of my greatest joys. However, in my early leadership years, I had an experience that threatened to derail me from developing people. I hired a staff member who was gifted with great potential, and I developed him wholeheartedly for months, then released him to lead. But then he broke my trust, and I had to let him go.

I was crushed. I felt the pain of losing everything I had put into developing this young leader, and on top of that, I felt I had also lost a friend. So I decided to stop investing in others emotionally and professionally. I was disengaged for six months, and I became miserable. Not only that, my leadership suffered and so did my team. It took some time, but I realized that disconnecting was an even bigger mistake than developing someone and failing. Yes, developing other leaders can be

It's very difficult for people to rise up if their leader refuses to put the wind of development under their wings.

hit-and-miss. I learned to live with that because the downside of not developing people is much greater than the relatively small losses that come from giving people a chance to reach their potential. It's very difficult for people to rise up if their leader refuses to put the wind of development under their wings.

CREDIBILITY AS A DEVELOPER OF PEOPLE

Your ability to develop others is dependent on what you know and what you are able to do. But it's equally dependent on *who you are*. Development is caught as much at it is taught. The catching part is totally dependent upon your credibility.

Earlier in this chapter I shared a list of the people who developed me, along with many of the lessons they taught me. However, they did much more than just *teach* me. Yes, I benefited intellectually from their wisdom, but it was my heart that caught their spirit. They shaped me by being who they were. I started to adopt their values and character traits. They were contagious in the transference of their positive qualities. I "caught" . . .

- *Consistency* from my father
- *Faithfulness* from Elmer Towns
- *Reflectiveness* from Lon Woodrum
- *Duty* from Bob Kline
- *Creativity* from Les Parrott
- *Humility* from Tom Phillippe
- *Joy* from Orval Butcher

- *Fulfillment* from J. Oswald Sanders
- *Perspective* from Fred Smith
- *Focus* from Larry Maxwell
- *Vision* from Bill Bright
- *Reciprocity* from Zig Ziglar
- *Opportunity* from Sealy Yates
- *Servanthood* from Les Stobbe
- *Intentionality* from John Wooden

These leaders poured into my life and invested themselves in me, and I am grateful. And even now, in my mid-seventies, I still seek out people to learn from and inspire me to keep improving.

As you prepare to become a developer of people, you need to think about what you have to offer. The more wisdom and experience you have as a leader, the better your potential to invest in others by developing them. But even if you're relatively inexperienced, as long as you are open, authentic, learning, and growing, you will be able to develop others. To gauge where you currently stand, ask yourself these three questions:

What is My Level of Credibility?

Credibility is everything to the people you desire to develop. No one asks to be coached by a person who's never demonstrated success. No one seeks business advice from a person who's never run a successful business. No one gets fitness instruction from someone who is out of shape. No one asks a mediocre speaker to coach them in communication. It just doesn't make sense.

My friend Dale Bronner, a very successful businessman and pastor who has served on my nonprofit board for years, wrote a book on mentoring, and I love the way he described credibility in a mentor:

Mentors have what the French call "savoir-faire." The literal translation of *savoir* is "to know," and *faire* means "to do." Consequently, savoir-faire means "knowing how to do."

The term has often been applied to individuals who are cultured in etiquette—"She has a certain savoir-faire."

Mentors, too, must possess a specific know-how. Without this confidence and knowledge, they are not ready to transfer what they've learned to others.[2]

As you begin developing people, give from whatever you have. Help people in the areas where you have demonstrated success. And keep growing! The more you learn and develop yourself today, the more you will have to give others tomorrow. As your credibility grows, you can expand the areas in which you develop others.

WILL MY STRENGTHS CONTRIBUTE TO THEIRS?

Before you engage in a mentoring relationship, it's important that you know this truth: we teach what we know, but we reproduce who we are. The reason development is so powerful is that good leaders possess the ability to reproduce their abilities in the lives of the people they develop, but that is only possible if the developers and those they develop share similar strengths.

It's fine to admire talented and accomplished people. It's great to partner with them if there's something you can accomplish together. But if you don't have common strengths, a mentoring relationship isn't going to be highly successful. The leader will become frustrated, and the person being developed won't be capable of executing what the leader teaches. It would be like LeBron James trying to teach basketball to a five-foot-eight couch potato. So begin developing others by focusing on using your strengths to develop similar strengths in them. You don't need to try to be all things to someone you develop. We all need multiple mentors and coaches.

The two areas where I mentor and coach people most are leadership and communication, because those are my greatest strengths. And the people I work with have ability in one or both of those areas. So when they ask questions, they are often very specific or highly complex, and it gives me great joy to share from my fifty-plus years of experience. The more skilled and experienced they are, the more competent questions they ask. That's as it should be.

WHAT EXPERIENCES OUTSIDE MY STRENGTHS CAN I GIVE THEM?

Obviously, the people you develop will need more than you can provide. They will need development in areas where you lack talent or experience. So what should you do, since you cannot give what you do not have? Become a facilitator of experiences for them. Give them books to read. Send them to classes or seminars. Connect them to other leaders with strengths you lack. Much of people development is hands-on; you must be willing to give your personal time and effort to it. But you can arrange some of it *for* people using resources you possess at your disposal.

AN ATTITUDE OF ADDING VALUE

Becoming a developer of people is really about looking for ways to add value to others every day and committing to follow through. Someone who does that is my friend Sheri Riley. She is an author, a speaker, and a Maxwell Leadership certified coach, and the founder and president of Exponential Living. Fresh out of the University of Louisville with a degree in business administration, she dreamed of working in the entertainment industry. She was hired by Trevel Productions, the management company of singer, songwriter, and producer Gerald Levert. A few years later, she became senior marketing director for LaFace Records. That's when she began actively developing people. She mentored her first assistant, a young woman named Tashion Macon, and helped her become a product manager. Tashion went on to earn a PhD in psychology and become a principal in her own marketing agency.

She invested in the first artist she was assigned to work with, a fifteen-year-old kid who had just been signed to the record label. She instantly saw that he had extraordinary talent, and she was blown away by his charisma. She had heard plenty of horror stories about young people in the music business whose lives were wrecked by early fame and fortune. She didn't want to see that happen to him. Sheri determined to be like a big sister to him, someone who would mentor him and tell him the truth—not what he wanted to hear. She wanted to help him build a firm foundation for a long and successful career.

Just in case you're wondering, that fifteen-year-old kid was Usher. And he's had a respected, highly successful career. He has sold more than 75 million records,[3] multiple dozens of his songs have made it onto the *Billboard* charts, and nine songs have gone to number one.[4] Usher said of Sheri:

> I immediately sensed something unusual about her. Her humanity. She was interested in me not just as a marketing project but as a whole person. She asked me questions and *really listened* to my answers, with no hidden agendas.
>
> Sheri soon became my friend and life consultant. Sometimes she was like a mother to me, sometimes like a big sister, sometimes like a coach. But she always had my back, and I always trusted her implicitly.[5]

Today Sheri is an empowerment speaker who spends much of her time communicating to corporate audiences in the United States and internationally, but her greatest passion is still developing and coaching people. Her primary focus is on helping athletes, entertainers, coaches, and corporate executives to grow personally and dominate professionally.

That's what developers do. They don't just lead a team and strive for organizational success. They invest in people to help them improve their lives. And when it comes time to train, coach, and mentor those people who have benefited from their investment, they are more open to following them and learning even more.

If you desire to develop leaders in your organization or on your team, the way to start is to commit to becoming a developer of people. That's the strong foundation upon which to build.

ACTION STEPS

1. Who are the people who have invested in you? Make a list and beside the names write what you learned from them. This will help you begin thinking about your own development and the process you went though. Write notes on what worked well and what was especially significant to you. You may also want to write thank-you notes to some of the people on that list.

---

2. Up until now, how committed have you been to developing others? As evidence, write the names of people you have developed and what you did to invest in them. If you have not developed people, which of the obstacles to developing others has been a hindrance to you?

   - **Lack of Awareness**
   - **Lack of Time**
   - **Inability to Find Someone to Develop**
   - **Lack of Belief in Others**
   - **Reluctance Due to Past Failures**

   What must you to do overcome those obstacles in the future? Write a plan to do that.

3. How would you assess your credibility as a developer of people? Write a profile of yourself (for your eyes only). What are your professional successes? What professional and personal activities have given you

experience and wisdom? What are your strengths? What do you have to offer that can add value to others?

---

4. Make a list of the people on your team. If you do not have a formal leadership position, list the names of people with whom you have influence. Think about each person and try to discern how you could add value to him or her. In particular, try to focus on how you can use your strengths and experience to improve their strengths. Write down how you might be able to help them. Immediately begin looking for opportunities to do that with no strings attached or expectation of a return.

THREE

GET TO KNOW YOUR
TEAM MEMBERS

In 2004, the Coca-Cola Company was in trouble. According to business consultant Gregory Kesler, the company faced "health-conscious consumers who were saying 'no' to carbonated soft drinks, stagnant new product creation, years of cuts in direct marketing, a stock price that had been pummeled for more than four years, and a business press that had pronounced 'the fizz was gone' from the Coke formula."[1] In response to these challenges, on May 4, 2004, Coca-Cola announced that retired executive Neville Isdell would return to the company and become its new chairman and CEO.

Isdell had spent more than thirty years at Coca-Cola and despite his success, he had never before been considered for the CEO position. But he accepted it as "the ultimate challenge."[2] On his first day back at Coca-Cola headquarters in Atlanta, he didn't take action. Instead, he told the employees, "It's all about you. It's all about the people."[3] In an interview several years later, Isdell said, "I made it clear that I was here to take long-term action, and that I wanted to go out and listen and communicate before making a lot of changes."[4] To accomplish that, he went on a listening tour. He connected with the key leaders on his team to understand them and their problems firsthand. He said, "We joked that the company had become a 'feedback-free zone,' and we knew that had to change."[5]

Three months later, Isdell gathered his direct reports plus the top 150 executives of Coca-Cola in London, determined to get their input for a plan to take the company forward. Isdell said:

> We were going to develop a total growth plan for the company, not just new strategies and a mission statement. . . . It would be a road map for how to get the company growing again and sustain that growth over the long term. It would not be dictated from on high but developed organically by the company's top leaders. . . . As the meetings progressed, and the executives began to realize that they really were able to shape the future of the company, the enthusiasm grew exponentially.[6]

Isdell was able to get Coke going in the right direction again. And while he did it, he actively prepared his successor. He helped his organization and everyone in it because he connected to his team members, listened to them, and benefited from their knowledge and experience.

START BY LISTENING

In *The Contrarian's Guide to Leadership*, Steven B. Sample wrote, "The average person suffers from three delusions: (1) that he is a good driver, (2) that he has a good sense of humor, and (3) that he is a good listener. Most people, however, including many leaders, are terrible listeners; they actually think talking is more important than listening."[7]

I once heard a joke that said we hear half of what is being said, listen to half of what we hear, understand half of that, believe half of that, and remember only half of that. If you translate those assumptions into an eight-hour workday, here is what it would mean:

You spend about four hours listening.

You hear about two hours of what is said.

You actually listen to an hour of that.

You *understand* only thirty minutes of that.

You *believe* only fifteen minutes of that.

And you remember only seven and a half minutes of it.

No wonder so few people are getting anything done.

Listening is one of the most important skills any leader can possess, yet most of us put greater emphasis on talking. Psychiatrist and author David D. Burns observed, "The biggest mistake you can make in trying to talk convincingly is to put your highest priority on expressing your ideas and feelings. What most people really want is to be listened to, respected, and understood. The moment people see that they are being understood, they become more motivated to understand your point of view."[8]

How many times have you heard people complain that their bosses don't listen? How many times have you heard children say their parents don't listen? People in authority usually prefer to talk. However, there is perhaps no better way to get to know others and connect with them than to become a better listener.

LISTENING LEADS TO UNDERSTANDING PEOPLE

The biggest communication challenge for many leaders is that most of the time we do not listen to understand. We listen to prepare our reply. Author and negotiation expert Herb Cohen said, "Effective listening requires more than hearing the words transmitted. It demands that you find meaning and understanding in what is being said. After all, meanings are not in words, but in people."[9]

People who understand one another work better together. And leaders are always more effective leading people they understand and care about. That process starts with listening.

LISTENING IS THE BEST WAY TO LEARN

Television host Larry King said, "I remind myself every morning: nothing I say this day will teach me anything. So, if I'm going to learn, I must do it by listening."[10] When we fail to listen, we shut off much of our learning potential.

The higher you go in leadership, the more likely people will be to tell you what you want to hear instead of what you need to know. The day before Dwight Eisenhower became president of the United States, outgoing president Harry Truman is said to have told him, "This is the last day people will be honest with you."

If you want to be an effective leader, you must make learning by listening a top priority every day. You can't become impatient just because you like to see results. What others have to say to you really must remain more important than what you have to say to them—not only because the higher leaders rise, the farther they get from the front lines, but also because you can't get to know people if you won't listen to them. Listening is the best way to gather information, to learn, to understand people, and to connect with them.

LISTENING ENGENDERS TRUST AND CONNECTION

Leaders who genuinely listen and keep confidences gain the trust of the people they work with. As a young leader I didn't have trouble keeping confidences, but I did have trouble listening. I was more interested in moving my agenda forward than listening to the people on my team. Only when a team member confronted me about my poor listening did I finally understand I had a problem. Not surprisingly, I probably would have understood it earlier if I'd been *listening* to people. Others had probably been trying to tell me for a long time, but I just didn't hear it. When this team member finally got through to me, I realized what she was really telling me was that I wasn't trustworthy. She believed her ideas, opinions, and feelings were not safe with me. I had to earn her trust. That started when I become a better listener.

Author and professor David Augsburger said, "Being heard is so close to being loved that for the average person, they are almost indistinguishable."[11] Listening draws people to you, which works much better than trying to push your leadership on them. Empathy builds trust; trust gives opportunities to develop others.

> "Being heard is so close to being loved that for the average person, they are almost indistinguishable."
>
> —DAVID AUGSBURGER

You can never get the best out of people if you don't know who they are, where they want to go, what they care about, how they think, and how they want to contribute. You can learn those things only if you listen. When that happens, people feel that they are at the very heart of things. They feel like partners, not just employees. They trust you more because you care about them.

As a leader, one of the most important things you can do with people you want to develop is understand and connect with them. And it's important to remember that's a two-way street. Yes, you want to understand that potential leader. But you always want to offer that person opportunities to better understand you.

ALWAYS ASK QUESTIONS

Once you become a better listener, you can increase your understanding of people by asking questions. I'm a talker, so it took me a while to learn this. As I learned to ask more questions, I made an important discovery. Asking questions has the opposite effect of giving direction. When you give direction to your team, you often confine them. When you ask questions, you create room for discovery—for articulation, communication, innovation, and problem-solving. Questions show that you know you don't have all the answers and value the input of others. Here are other things questions do:

- Create space for open conversation
- Place value on others and their opinions
- Help people know one another better
- Invite everyone to participate
- Clear up assumptions
- Cause people to think
- Guide the conversation

When we face the fact that none of us knows all the answers and all of us will make mistakes, we create a culture where creativity can flourish, mistakes are acceptable, and people learn from setbacks.

Recently a leader expressed his frustration to me when I was encouraging him to ask more questions instead of giving more direction to his team. "If I ask questions," he said, "I cannot control the response that is given." But leadership isn't control—it's influence. I tried to help him understand that you don't want to control people's responses. You want to influence their thinking and actions. You do that by asking the right questions. The questions you ask guide the direction and the pace. The deeper the questions go, the deeper their understanding of leadership— and your understanding of them. Questions can actually enhance your leadership, not undermine it.

Asking questions helps leaders build relationships. When I started asking questions, I did it to gain information. But in the process, I learned that I got to know people better. Because I understood them better, I was able to lead them better. And they become more open to my investment in them.

Too often as leaders, we lead by assumption. What a mistake. As Simon Sinek said in his book *Start with Why*:

> We make decisions based on what we *think* we know. It wasn't too long ago that the majority of people believed the world was flat. This perceived truth impacted behavior. During this period, there was very little exploration. People feared that if they traveled too far they might fall off the edge of the earth. So, for the most part they stayed put. It wasn't until that minor detail was revealed—the world is round—that behaviors changed on a massive scale. Upon this discovery, societies began to traverse the planet. Trade routes were established; spices were traded. New ideas, like mathematics, were shared between societies which unleashed all kinds of innovations and advancements. The correction of a simple false assumption moved the human race forward.[12]

When I finally started asking questions instead of making assumptions, it improved every aspect of my leadership. As you prepare to develop potential leaders, I suggest that you start using questions as bookends for every meeting.

FRONT-END QUESTIONS

As a developer of people, you need to be looking ahead. You need to see more than others see and before others see. You need to maximize the time you spend with your team members. Here are some examples of questions I ask team members as we approach a project, engage in an experience, or have a mentoring conversation:

"What is your response to the vision we're proposing?"
"How do you think we should approach this project?"
"What do you expect to receive from this experience?"
"How do you think this conversation will play out?"

The more open-ended the questions, the more you can learn about how someone thinks. And the more difficult, intuitive, or abstract the subject, the more talent and experience is needed to answer it. You find out a lot about people by how they answer. Every time you ask someone to evaluate the leadership dynamics of a situation, their answer tells you a lot about their leadership potential.

BACK-END QUESTIONS

I love asking questions that prompt team members to evaluate and reflect on their experiences. I want to gauge their level of awareness. I want to know what they observed. I want to know how they felt. I want to know what they learned. I want to know how they will apply it. I want to find out what actions they plan to take next. Good questions asked on the back end can often prompt people to make discoveries and learn for themselves. And if they miss the lesson, you can always take a moment to teach them.

Asking questions will always serve you well. Front-end questions *set* the agenda, while back-end questions *maximize* the agenda. Front-end questions encourage preparation, while back-end questions encourage reflection. Both kinds of questions increase understanding. And they pave the way for more effective leadership, and leadership development in others.

> Front-end questions *set* the agenda, while back-end questions *maximize* the agenda. Front-end questions encourage preparation, while back-end questions encourage reflection.

THE GOAL:
SEE THE WORLD FROM THEIR PERSPECTIVE

Good leadership requires a perspective shift from *it's all about me* to *it's all about others*. That means we need to try to see things from others' points of view. Steffan Surdek, consulting principal, trainer, and coach at Pyxis Technologies, said, "Perspective is the way individuals see the world. It comes from their personal point of view and is shaped by life experiences, values, their current state of mind, the assumptions they bring into a situation, and a whole lot of other things. . . . We can easily say that my perspective is my reality."[13]

If you want to develop the members of your team as people and then be able to develop them as leaders, you need to get to know them. You need to learn how to see the world from their perspectives. How can you do that?

LEARN PERSPECTIVE THINKING

I wish I had tried to think the way others do earlier in my leadership career. For too long I simply wanted others to think the way I did, and I couldn't understand why they didn't. So, I spent a lot of time and energy trying to persuade them to adopt my perspective. But that's not a good way to build relationships. Slowly I began to learn how others thought and to lead them from where they were, not from where I was. I recommend you do the same.

PRACTICE PERSPECTIVE SEEKING

Frequently after a meeting, I will ask the leaders from my team to give their perspective and their takeaways on what happened. Their comments help me catch things I may have missed. They also give me insight into their understanding of the dynamics that occurred in the room. Often when I'm developing someone, I'll get their perspective and then give them mine. Sometimes I'm able to teach them something and help them go further in their leadership journey.

ENGAGE IN PERSPECTIVE COORDINATING

Whenever I get together with my team, whether it's in a planning time to achieve an objective, a review after we hold an event, or a debriefing meeting after meeting with another organization, as I've already said, I seek out my team members' perspectives. But I don't stop there. The real value in the conversation comes from coordinating those perspectives with one another. I do that by pointing out how one team member's ideas relate to the others'. I also tell them how those ideas relate to my thinking. And I try to tie all of it together to the vision of our organization.

I'm trying to do more than just get to know them. I'm working to expand everyone's vision and perspective. I'm trying to help them sharpen their leadership thinking. I'm trying to help them get to know one another. And I'm making it possible for us to come up with a new shared perspective that makes all of us better. It benefits us individually, improves our team, and prompts everyone to process ideas and think more broadly, not just from their own perspective. That in itself is also part of their development process.

EARLY DEVELOPMENT SUCCESS

One of my early successes in people development was Barbara Brumagin. She became my assistant in 1981. She not only became a successful and indispensable part of my team, but she grew into a terrific leader. While I was working on this book, I asked her to share some of her observations from those early days. Here's one of the things Barbara said about those experiences:

> On day one of my employment, my desk in the office was arranged so I could see and hear you in your adjoining office. You had more than an open-door policy. I was able to observe how you worked at your desk—doing both the mundane and the critical, developing daily and long-term planning, and interacting with people. Any time you had a significant encounter, you took time to teach me your thought process, give me background, and tell me why and how you formed a decision; it helped me understand and prepared me for any related task assigned to me. . . .
>
> At a time when assistants were not included in an organization's weekly planning meetings, you brought me into those meetings. That helped prepare me for new tasks, understand projects, and know what team members needed from you or me. And following these meetings, you always asked if I had any questions or feedback, or if I needed clarification. You asked what I observed and learned. You valued my thoughts and provided me with an opportunity to understand your assessment process. Any time we met, I knew I would always have an opportunity to ask questions.
>
> And you always thanked me. Nearly every conversation ended with your saying, "Thank you for helping me." To this day when we speak on the phone, your last words are "Is there anything I can do for you?"

Barbara was a great work partner with me. I can't tell you how much she helped me during the eleven years we worked together. She started as my assistant, but she became so much more. Because I understood her, and I was open with her and intentional about helping her understand me, she took more and more on her shoulders. She became able to communicate for me and make decisions in my place. That was possible only because we knew each other so well.

If you are going to develop people, you need to learn who they are and do everything you can to understand them. And you need to be open enough to allow them to understand and learn from you.

And while you do that, be sure to encourage them. While people's hopes and dreams may be unique, they all need to be encouraged and lifted up. Here's what I've discovered:

- Most people are insecure. Give them confidence.
- Most people want to feel special. Compliment them.
- Most people want a bright future. Give them hope.
- Most people need to be understood. Listen to them.
- Most people want direction. Walk with them.
- Most people are selfish. Speak to their needs first.
- Most people get emotionally low. Encourage them.
- Most people want to be included. Ask their opinion.
- Most people want success. Help them win.
- Most people want to be appreciated. Give them credit.

When you understand how people think, meet them where they are, and encourage them, they will be willing to learn from you. And they have a greater chance of being developed as leaders in the future.

ACTION STEPS

1. How good are you at listening? If Steven B. Sample is right, most people consider themselves to be good listeners even when they aren't. Decide what score you would give yourself out to ten (with ten being the highest). Then talk to five people who know you well and ask them how they would score you. This will give you a baseline for your listening ability.

---

2. If your listening scores were lower than nines or tens, you have work to do to become a better listener. Identify three situations or settings where you typically listen less than you could. Create a plan for listening, understanding, and retaining information in those situations. If necessary, use the skill of restating what others say and asking if you heard correctly. If not, ask the speaker for clarification and try again.

---

3. The next time you meet with one or more team members, use the front-end/back-end questions method to better get to know them. Write down your front-end questions before meeting to make sure you're prepared. When the meeting is done, ask debriefing and opinion questions before everyone disperses. If you think you will have difficulty recalling people's answers, take notes.

---

4. Make an effort to gain the perspective of each of your team members. Ask which parts of their job they love. Ask which parts they find most challenging and why. Get their opinions about the work

the team does and how it contributes to the organization. Ask about their hopes and dreams for the future. As you engage them, don't judge or challenge their responses. Listen and learn.

FOUR

EQUIP TEAM MEMBERS TO EXCEL AT THEIR JOBS

All leaders want to achieve their organizational goals, and most are aware they can accomplish them only when their teams excel. They understand that what President Ronald Reagan said was true: "The greatest leader is not necessarily the one who does the greatest things. He is the one that gets the people to do the greatest things."

Not all leaders approach this objective the same way. Some rely on their ability to communicate their vision. Others work to fire up enthusiasm in team members. Many criticize team members, pointing out their weaknesses. Or they pit them against one another. But as USC professor Morgan McCall said, "Survival of the fittest is not the same as survival of the best." Others set out incentives hoping people will reach for them. The worst leaders threaten people. But as President Dwight D. Eisenhower said, "You don't lead by hitting people over the head— that's assault, not leadership."

Over the years, I've found that there are three main reasons people fail in a job. They may lack the ability or the desire to do the job. Or they are not properly trained to do the job. Or they do not understand what they are supposed to do to complete the job. The good news is that equipping addresses two out of three of those problems. If team members who possess ability and desire fail, you may be at fault because you neglected to train them properly.

LEARNING TO EQUIP OTHERS

When I started my leadership journey, I relied on charisma and hard work to move the organization forward. In my first position as a pastor, I gathered plenty of followers, but I did nearly everything myself. I was young and energetic, so I was able to keep that up for the three years I spent in that position. But when I moved on, everything I had left behind fell apart. That's when I realized that the function of leadership isn't to gather more followers. It's to produce more leaders. But you can't always start by asking people to lead. You need to give them a track to run on. The place to start is by equipping them to excel at their jobs. Not only does this propel the organization forward, but it also gives them experience and successes which create a credibility from which they can later lead.

> If team members who possess ability and desire fail, you may be at fault because you neglected to train them properly.

So, in the second organization I led, I started working to equip my people. The way I started was simple; I never worked alone. If I was taking on a task, I invited people to join me so they could learn to do it too. If I launched a project, others worked alongside me. If I went out on a call to visit someone, a companion went with me. Soon, others

were capable of doing anything I could do. And
they started helping me. As they took over my
tasks, I took on new ones.

> The function of
> leadership isn't to
> gather more followers.
> It's to produce
> more leaders.

That's when I started to experience the
power of multiplication. As I equipped the
people working with me, helping them become
great at their jobs, I began experiencing the compounding of influence, time, energy, resources,
ideas, money, and effectiveness. I discovered that many hands really do
make light work, as the old saying goes.

As people learned to do their jobs well and rose up, it became easy
to identify the potential leaders in the group. But as I continued to train
team members, I realized I was still missing something. The people I
equipped were helping me lift my load of leadership, but if I failed to
train *them* to equip and develop *others*, we would not be able to take the
organization to higher levels of success.

Having more trained team members and more equipped leaders
meant being able to accomplish more with what we had. It meant we
could start new initiatives. It meant we had an army of people solving
problems and overcoming obstacles. Not only that, but I found that
equipping leaders could free me up to put more of my time into those
areas that provided the highest return for me and my organizations. (In
the next several chapters, I'll teach you how to identify *your* potential
leaders, bring them into a leadership environment, and develop them.
Before you can develop leaders, you need a pool of trained, successful
team members.)

Inspired by this greater vision, I worked on creating a new equipping model. It needed to be something not only that I could do and
teach but also that every person in the organization could understand,
practice, and teach to others. Here's what I came up with:

I do it.

I do it and you are with me.

You do it and I am with you.

You do it.

You do it and someone else is with you.

You can see that this process starts with the leader who intends to equip others. First, that leader needs to be successful. As soon as you know what you're doing, invite team members to join you and let them watch you. In the third step, the focus moves away from the leader: it goes from *I* to *you*. At that point, others are doing the task, and the leader coaches, encourages, and corrects the people doing the work. After that is the handoff. The task is delegated to the equipped team member. But importantly, there is a fifth step. The person who has been trained selects another team member to train. This is where the effectiveness transforms—it goes from addition to multiplication. If every team member trains someone else, the multiplication factor never stops. We put this model to work in my nonprofit organization EQUIP when training leaders from 1997 to 2016. In those years, EQUIP trained five million leaders from every country in the world.

As a leader, it's one thing to ask people be on your team and take a journey with you. It's another to equip them with a roadmap for the trip. Good leaders provide a means for people on the team to get where they need to go. They equip and empower them. As soon as I realized the positive impact that equipping could make, I changed my focus. And my leadership took a giant leap. Yours can too.

THINK LIKE AN EQUIPPING LEADER

My desire is to help you establish an equipping mind-set as a leader. This will allow you to give your team greater horsepower and help you to see who the racehorses are. What does it mean to have an equipper's mind-set?

I imagine it as being similar to preparing people to climb Mount Everest. First of all, you have to assess the level of potential in each person. Are they out-of-shape couch potatoes? Are they fit but inexperienced? Are they experienced but out of shape? Do they possess a great base of experience and fitness but need to be made ready to go to the next level? As the team's leader, you need to know.

You must assess what equipment will be needed for the climb. What are the conditions? What have you learned from making the same climb yourself? Where are the dangers and pitfalls? What do people need to know that you know? And how can you help them start thinking like a mountain climber? Can you teach them to look at the peak and assess how it should be conquered? Because as an equipping leader, it's not enough to just get them up and down the mountain without freezing to death. Ultimately, you want them to learn how to climb the mountain and gain the skills to guide *others* up the mountain by teaching those people everything you taught. Your goal is to equip people in such a way that they learn not only to do their job well, but to lead and to develop their own equipping leader's mind-set.

ESSENTIALS FOR EQUIPPING

As I reflect on all the ways I have equipped people over the years, I believe you can be successful in the process if you focus on five essential practices.

1. BE AN EXAMPLE OTHERS WANT TO FOLLOW

You've probably noticed that I often emphasize the importance of setting the right example. Why? Because you will never have enough credibility or skills to develop others if you are not developing yourself as a leader. I have another handy acronym to help you with this: LEAD. Here is what you need to be asking yourself:

Learning: "What am I learning?"
Experiencing: "What am I experiencing?"
Applying: "What am I applying?"
Developing: "Who am I developing?"

> Telling others to do what you haven't done yourself isn't equipping. It's bossing.

Telling others to do what you haven't done yourself isn't equipping. It's bossing. When you learn, experience, apply, and *then* develop others, that's not bossing; it's leading.

I like what content strategist and writer Steve Olenski wrote about this in *Forbes*:

An employee will see the value of the development process when they see their current leadership continue to develop personally and professionally. By modeling this behavior, leaders build credibility and the trust necessary to encourage employees to participate in development-building activities. It shows employees that development is part of the organization's culture. It sends the message that it's important for, and expected from, everyone in the organization to be part of a continual improvement process that nurtures from within.[1]

Coaches in my organizations have trained people in large and small corporations across the United States and in every stream of influence in nations around the world: government, business, arts, education, faith, media, sports, and healthcare. The number one factor in determining if any kind of training course is successful in an organization is whether or not its senior leaders are involved. If they show that learning is a priority to them by fully participating in the training process, it is successful. If they are not involved, the people in the organization conclude it's that not important. The leaders' absence creates a credibility gap.

If you want to train team members and eventually develop leaders, you need credibility. If you are growing and developing, they will respect you—even if you're not far ahead of them in the journey. So keep learning, and model personal development.

2. Spend Time with Your Team Members

All the equipping models that I have practiced since 1974 have one thing in common: the Proximity Principle. I bring the people close to me to equip and invest in them. You can't do it from a distance. The closer team members are to you, the more interactions they will have with you and the more lessons they will receive.

This can be a challenge in a virtual working environment. You can try to simulate proximity using technology, but I don't believe it has the same effect. So if that's your situation, you need to create touch points with your team. You need to arrange times when you can work together in the same location, even if it's for a few hours or a few days.

What's wonderful about the Proximity Principle is that anyone can practice it. You don't need any experience as an equipper or trainer. You don't have to be a high-level leader. It doesn't require a formal leadership position.

The most important words a leader speaks to others are "Follow me." When I ask people to join me and they stay close, they can see me in action and learn from me. They can understand what I do and why. We can share the experience together. They can ask questions. There is no substitute for intentional proximity.

3. Set Equipping Goals with Them

At some point in the equipping process, you need to set goals for your team members. You can do it as you invite them into the development process, or you can start them in the development process to get a better understanding of them and then pause to set objectives. But you need to do it, because the goals become a roadmap for them to follow. As you do, use the following guidelines to help you.

Tailor the Goals to the Person

You already know some things about the person you're going to equip, because you've taken the time to ask questions. There are things you need or want accomplished by someone on your team. Plus, you probably have an intuitive sense of the person's potential. Put those things together to create goals for people, and ask yourself and the team, "Are these goals a right fit for you?"

Make the Goals Attainable

Nothing is more discouraging than being given goals that are unachievable. It's being set up to fail. You need to put your team members on a success track. I like what Ian MacGregor, former AMAX chairman of the board, said about this: "I work on the same principles as people who train horses. You start with low fences, easily achieved goals, and work up. It's important in management never to ask people to try to accomplish goals they can't accept."[2] Let them start small and work their way up. Help them get some wins under their belt.

Create Goals That Require Them to Stretch

Just because your team members need to start small doesn't mean they should stay small. Ideally, every goal should require them to reach and grow to achieve it. And with each succeeding goal, they should be able to reach farther and grow further. By the time they have accomplished all the goals you set together, they will be able to look back and be surprised by the progress they've made and the growth they've experienced.

Make the Goals Measurable

It's not enough to say, "I want to get better," or "I want to grow as a leader." Those are good desires, and they may provide direction, but they are not goals. Every goal you identify for team members needs to be specific enough that you and they can clearly answer yes or no to the question, "Did you achieve this goal?"

Make the Goals Clear and in Writing

Finally, ask the team member to put the goals in writing. This way, the goals become specific, and the potential leader becomes accountable.

Putting together a game plan gives each person a track to run on. For any new team members, check in frequently to discuss how they are doing achieving their goals. The more experienced people become, the more of a long-term process equipping becomes, until it shifts more into a mentoring relationship, which we'll discuss in chapter 11.

4. Encourage Team Members to Learn by Doing

I've been told that in hospital emergency rooms, nurses have a saying, "Watch one, do one, teach one." In other words, new nurses follow experienced nurses and watch what they do. Then the new nurses do the same thing. They are expected to turn around and teach someone else. In the fast pace of the medical profession, nurses are encouraged to jump right in on the job, practice new skills, and then pass them on. Few things cement learning like actually doing the work yourself, hands on. Theory and instruction alone produce limited results. The moment people get involved, their abilities rise quickly.

Research supports this idea. Industrial psychologist Robert Eichinger, along with Michael Lombardo and Morgan McCall, developed what they called the 70/20/10 learning and development model in the 1990s. It says that 70 percent of the time, learning and development occur in the context of real-life and on-the-job experiences, tasks, and problem-solving; 20 percent of the time, they come from informal or formal feedback, mentoring, or coaching from other people; and 10 percent of the time, they result from formal training.[3] If you want to equip people, stay close to them and coach them while allowing them to gain hands-on experience doing things that will expand them and prompt them to grow.

A lot of times leaders are reluctant to let people with little experience take on tasks because they fear tasks will be done poorly. But my answer to this is to pick when and how you hand off equipping experiences. Start people with less important tasks, especially when they're new, and let them work their way up to more difficult challenges. And when they do move up to more important responsibilities, touch base with them often to see how they're doing, answer questions, and give encouragement. The more experience they gain, the less contact you need with them.

One of my sweet spots as a leader is communication, and I frequently have opportunities to equip people to become better communicators. I can't do that by simply talking, because telling is not equipping, and listening doesn't mean learning. People learn by doing. Take a look at the difference in approach I could take to helping a young communicator:

- "Emma, I'd like you to give a five-minute talk next Thursday night." In this case, I'm telling Emma what to do. I'm giving her a task.
- "Emma, prepare your five-minute talk by writing it out, then

practicing it." I've added some specific explanation to help her, but I'm still only teaching.

- "Emma, let's get together. You practice delivering the talk to me. Then we'll discuss how you can improve it." I'm interacting with Emma, but she's doing the work and gaining experience.
- "Emma, let's get together, and you can show me what adjustments you've made to the talk and practice delivering it to me again." I've given her an opportunity to gain more experience.
- "Emma, I want you to deliver your talk Thursday night. I'll give you feedback afterward." Now I've maximized the experience for her.

In this example, Emma did all the work herself, but I've set her up for success by giving her guidance on the front end, coaching in the middle, the invaluable experience of delivering the communication with a live audience, and giving her feedback at the end.

You need to pick your spots for training people, but as you do, remember these two things: you need to let them learn by doing, and you need to be close enough to them to coach them along the way.

5. Remove Barriers to Growth

The final piece of the equipping puzzle is making ways for people to grow and move forward. Sometimes that means giving them tools or providing the resources they need. Other times it means introducing them to people who can help them—inside and outside the organization. And it always means creating an environment that allows people to flourish.

As a leader in my organizations, I think of myself as a "lid lifter." I want to give people room to reach their potential. To facilitate that, I work to remove any lids holding them down. Steve Olenski said:

Many organizations are rigid in their organizational structure and processes, which can make it challenging to implement some cross-functional development and facilitate dynamic growth and high-performance training. It's up to the leadership to bridge silos, knock down walls, and design a system that encourages a fluid approach to learning and working. Today's generation of workers are used to change and enjoy open work environments that let them explore. Take the barriers away and watch people flourish.[4]

If you're a leader on your team or in your organization, you need to take responsibility for removing barriers for the people you develop. Don't give them responsibility without authority. Don't give them tasks without resources to accomplish them. Don't say you want them to grow but then simply tell them exactly how to do their work. Enable them to learn by doing. Don't tell them they are the organization's most appreciable asset while failing to appreciate them. Equip them to succeed, and then release them.

Equipping is a game changer. It transforms the individual team members who become better at their jobs, increase in their confidence, and see brighter futures for themselves. It transforms the team because it becomes more capable and productive. It adds value to the organization because the team contributes more to achieving the vision and adds to the bottom line. And it helps team leaders because they don't have to carry as many responsibilities themselves. The load is shared.

To become an effective equipper, you need to ask yourself some questions. Are you willing to pour your life into others? Are you willing to put in the time, commitment, and sacrifice it will require? Often, it's quicker and easier to do a job yourself than to train someone else to do it. But that's short-term thinking. The time you invest now will compound when well-equipped team members are working with you, and you begin to see who the potential leaders are. Recognizing them is the subject of the next chapter.

ACTION STEPS

1. Effective equippers are good role models. What are you currently, intentionally, and actively doing to grow personally and professionally? Specifically, how much time are you spending every day and every week on growth? How much money are you investing?

   If your answers to these questions are positive and specific, good job! Allow members of your team know it if you can do it without bragging.

   If your answers to those questions were not good, then you need to put yourself on a plan for growth. Begin reading books: as many as one a week but no fewer than one a month. Give yourself a goal of listening to a certain number of useful podcasts every month. Sign up for a workshop, conference, or certification course. Make growth a regular, ongoing, scheduled part of your life.

---

2. Begin practicing the Proximity Principle. Spend more time with your team members. Invite people along when you're doing your work so that they can observe you and learn from you. And whenever possible, follow this practice:

   I do it.
   I do it and you are with me.
   You do it and I am with you.
   You do it.
   You do it and someone else is with you.

---

3. Set equipping goals with each of your team members. Ask them what they want to learn. Tell them what you want them to learn—or learn to do better. Discuss any obstacles or barriers you or they foresee. Work on specific attainable goals for them that will require them to stretch and grow. Write out those goals with a timeline for completion. Take responsibility for removing obstacles to their growth.

---

4. Empower your team members to take action and learn by doing. But check in frequently with them to discuss their success and mistakes. Coach them, support them, and encourage them. Then release them to keep trying and learning. Keep working with them to achieve their goals by the agreed upon deadlines. Praise them privately and publicly when they succeed.

FIVE

IDENTIFY YOUR POTENTIAL LEADERS

One of my favorite activities when I speak is answering specific questions from the leaders in the audience. Recently, at a conference put on by Chick-fil-A, someone asked how I develop good leaders. "First," I responded, "you need to know what a leader looks like."

I know that may sound simplistic, but it's true. And I've found that most people have a difficult time describing what a potential leader looks like. Leadership experts and authors James M. Kouzes and Barry Z. Posner said, "Our images of who's a leader and who's not are all mixed up in our preconceived notions about what leadership is and isn't."[1] How can anyone find something they can't identify?

I read that when Jack Welch was the CEO of General Electric, he used to send out a memo to the incoming participants of the executive development course before they attended the first session. In it, he directed them to think about their answers to a group of questions that he wanted them to be ready to discuss. Here's what he wrote:

Tomorrow you are appointed CEO of GE:

- What would you do in the first thirty days?
- Do you have a current "vision" of what to do?
- How would you go about developing one?
- Present your best shot at the vision.
- How would you go about "selling" the vision?
- What foundations would you build on?
- What current practices would you jettison?[2]

During the development course, just hearing the participants' answers to these questions influenced Welch, giving him ideas about who his best potential leaders were. But years later, Welch also lamented his choice of successor, Jeff Immelt, who was a great talker and "the most polished politician" in a small group Welch considered selecting. Recalling an interview he had with Welch, William D. Cohan wrote:

> Mr. Immelt was a "know-it-all," Mr. Welch told me. "And you couldn't be a know-it-all and run a company that size [GE]. That's it in a nut-shell. He had the answer to everything. . . . If you want to pin failure on me, I missed it."[3]

Questions are good. I love asking questions. But that's not the whole answer. A great talker with poor potential might fool you. A poor talker with great potential might elude you. So, how do you do it?

OBSERVE TEAM MEMBERS YOU'VE EQUIPPED

Some leaders are tempted to recruit leaders from outside their organization and work with them. I recommend that you start where you are with who you have. Observe the members of your team, whom you should now know pretty well, since you've taken time to get to know them and equip them. Looking for potential leaders to develop in your own organization makes sense for three reasons:

1. They Are a Known Quantity

Unlike when you interview people from outside, you don't have to imagine how insiders will perform. You don't have to rely on what they say about themselves. You're not limited to hearing the opinions of their handpicked references. You can look at their actual performance to see what they can do. You can observe their strengths. You can personally talk to everyone who works with them to find out about them.

2. They Already Fit the Culture

Anytime you bring in someone from outside, you have to guess whether that person will really fit your culture and be able to work well with the people in your organization. When people have already been working in the organization for any length of time, you know if they fit because they have already been a part of the community.

3. They Have Already Established Influence

Good leaders, even those with little training or experience, influence other people. When you're trying to identify potential leaders to develop, look for influence. It's a qualification that must be present in someone you wish to develop as a leader, because leadership is influence, nothing more, nothing less. If people can't influence others, they won't be able to lead. And if they already have some degree of influence in your organization, they already possess an asset that they will be able to use in the future to get things done. It's like having a running head start in a race. When you give them tasks, they will be able to quickly mobilize the people they already influence.

How do you measure their influence? I recommend you use the 5 Levels of Leadership. Here they are in order from lowest to highest levels of influence:

1. **Position:** People follow because of title.
2. **Permission:** People follow because of relationships.
3. **Production:** People follow because of results.
4. **People Development:** People follow because of personal life change.
5. **Pinnacle:** People follow because of respect from earned reputation.

Andrew Carnegie was a master at identifying potential leaders. Once asked by a reporter how he had managed to hire forty-three millionaires, Carnegie responded that the men had not been millionaires when they started working for him. They had become millionaires as a result. The reporter next wanted to know how he had developed these men to become such valuable leaders. Carnegie replied, "Men are developed the same way gold is mined. . . . Several tons of dirt must be moved to get an ounce of gold; but you don't go into the mine looking for dirt," he added. "You go in looking for the gold."[4]

I wouldn't call the people who can't lead *dirt*, but I would definitely call the people who can *gold*. Where do you put your focus? On those who can't lead or on those who can—the *gold* within your organization?

No matter what kind of team, department, or organization you lead, you can find potential leaders to be developed. If you're not identifying the leaders of tomorrow whom you will develop, your potential and your future will always be limited.

A PICTURE OF POTENTIAL LEADERSHIP

As you look for potential leaders, remember that they will have the same characteristics as good leaders with whom you have already been working—except that they won't have *developed* these characteristics yet. You must try to see the potential oak in the seedling.

When I look for people with leadership potential, I start by examining five areas. I suggest you do the same as you observe your team members to see who the potential leaders are.

1. THE ATTITUDE OF POTENTIAL LEADERS: WILLING

Recently, I was having a conversation about hiring with my friend Ed Bastian, the CEO of Delta Airlines. Ed told me, "At Delta, we hire for attitude but train for aptitude. Always start with attitude." He continued, "Bring people on the team that the other members will enjoy working with."[5]

> "At Delta, we hire for attitude but train for aptitude. Always start with attitude. Bring people on the team that the other members will enjoy working with."
>
> —ED BASTIAN

Attitude is a choice, and at the heart of a good attitude is willingness—willingness to learn, to improve, to serve, to think of others, to add value, to do the right thing, and to make sacrifices for the team. Leadership skill may come from the head, but leadership attitude comes from the heart.

Good leaders want more *for* the people they lead than they want *from* them. For years I've taught potential leaders that people do not care about how much you know until they know how much you care. That means potential leaders must have empathy for others. And as Jeffrey Cohn and Jay Morgan said, "Empathy is critical for leadership for many reasons. Combined with integrity, it drives trust. It gives followers a sense that their interests are being looked after, and this creates positive energy. Followers who sense that a leader appreciates them are motivated to carry out their duties in a more committed way."[6]

When potential leaders have the right attitude, you can sense it. When their hearts are right, they have passion that spills out. They have energy. They're positive. They're like the chairman and CEO of Berkshire Hathaway, Warren Buffett, who loves what he does so much that he said, "I tap dance to work [every day]."[7] Or like longtime manager of the Los Angeles Dodgers Tommy Lasorda, who won two World Series titles. One night, after a crushing loss to Houston in the 1981 playoffs, Lasorda was undaunted and enthusiastic. When asked about his upbeat attitude, he said, "The best day of my life is when I manage a winning game. The second-best day of my life is when I manage a losing game."[8] That's the kind of attitude you want to see in the potential leaders you select to develop. They believe they can succeed. They're willing to put in the time and effort. Even in the face of defeat, they cheerfully keep working and trying to move forward.

2. The Character of Potential Leaders: Solid

A positive attitude is important. But good character is what holds together all the positive attitude traits I've mentioned—willingness to serve, selflessness, empathy, growth, and sacrifice. Character keeps everything secure. Without it, things can break down fast. Character is about managing your life well, so you can lead others well. As Gayle Beebe said, "The formation of our character creates predictability to our leadership. Predictability, dependability and consistency: these three qualities ensure that our leadership is reliable and motivates people to place their confidence in us. Our effectiveness as leaders is built on trust."[9]

> Character is about managing your life well, so you can lead others well.

When potential leaders have the right heart for people, choose to be positive every day, and maintain the good character to keep making the right choices, they possess the willingness needed to become better leaders. And they are *solid*. These are people you can trust and are worth choosing to develop.

3. THE ABILITY OF POTENTIAL LEADERS: HIGH

I already told you that Ed Bastian says at Delta they believe in hiring for attitude. But that doesn't mean he ignores talent. As he also told me, "We look for talent because talent lifts us." I'd add that leadership talent lifts organizations the most.[10]

Excellence is impossible in any endeavor without talent. No highly successful organization got to where it is without highly capable people. It isn't possible. Finding good leaders is like finding a good high jumper. It does you no good to find seven people who can jump one foot. You need one person who can jump seven feet. Leadership is too difficult and complex to be done by a committee of average people. The more difficult the situation, the higher the leaders must be able to "jump."

There is a saying that a person's gift makes room for him or her. Poet Ralph Waldo Emerson expressed a similar idea when he wrote, "Each man has his own vocation. The talent is the call. There is one direction in which all space is open to him."[11] The direction that has space for each of us is in our area of talent and giftedness. Not only are we able in that area—we are capable of becoming more able in that area.

How do you know potential leaders are gifted in a particular area?

- They will be good at it—that displays excellence.
- They will have opportunities to use it—that creates expansion.
- They will draw other people to them—that shows attraction.
- They will enjoy doing it—that brings fulfillment.

> "Talent is always conscious of its own abundance and does not object to sharing."
>
> —ALEKSANDR SOLZHENITSYN

Potential leaders with talent have the potential to lift the whole team or organization because of the excellence they achieve and to expand the organization through opportunity. That is a powerful combination, because, as Nobel laureate Aleksandr Solzhenitsyn observed, "Talent is always conscious of its own abundance and does not object to sharing."[12]

4. The Track Record of Potential Leaders: Proven

Talent is not always synonymous with achievement. That's why you need to examine the accomplishments of team members to see how much potential they have for leadership. You need to look at whether they have produced results in the past. Are they proven? What have they achieved? When given a task, do they complete it with excellence? Do they meet and exceed goals? Do they deliver? If they can produce results for themselves, they have the potential to help other people succeed. They can't lead others to success if they've never led themselves to it.

Good leaders come in all sizes, shapes, ages, and backgrounds. Their personalities are different, and they don't all lead the same way. However, people with the most leadership potential stand out from other people who are average because they know how to win.

5. The Mind-set of Potential Leaders: Improvement

The best leaders focus on improvement. They want to improve themselves, their products or services, individual team members, the team as a whole, and the organizations they're part of. In other words, they are builders. When I talk about builders, I mean people who share five characteristics:

Builders Are Seldom Satisfied

Builders don't get comfortable. They live the Law of the Rubber Band, which I taught in *The 15 Invaluable Laws of Growth*.[13] It says growth stops when you lose the tension between where you are and where you could be. Builders like to be stretched. Or as former Indy race car driver Mario Andretti said, "If everything seems under control, you're just not going fast enough."[14]

Builders Are Comfortable with Uncertainty

Change is constant and essential to progress, but change brings uncertainty. Builders are not uncomfortable with that. They know there are times when they must take steps forward without knowing all the answers or with limited information. But they move forward just the same, believing an answer exists, they can figure it out, and progress will result. After all, uncertainty is a leadership opportunity. The more uncertainty there is, the greater the need for good leaders to find the way and take others with them. Builders constantly seek ways to open doors and keep growing. They recognize that when nothing is 100 percent certain, anything is possible.

Builders Are Impatient

There are two kinds of progress in our world. There are things you must work for and things you must wait for. Builders excel in the progress that comes from working.

My friend Chris Hodges, who is definitely a builder, says that the vision gap is the space between what we *are* doing and what we *could* do. Builders are impatient to close that gap.

> The vision gap is the space between what we *are* doing and what we *could* do. Builders are impatient to close that gap.

Builders Are Contagious

Recently Maxwell Leadership began training people to become certified coaches in Poland. During the planning, Iwona Polkowska, one of our coaches from Poland, set up a launch call. A few minutes before we were scheduled to start, she and I were talking, and she told me more than a thousand people would be on the line. I was impressed and congratulated her, but Iwona was not. She said, "It's a start. You know there are thirty-eight million people in Poland." That got me excited, and I could see that Iwona was going to spread the word in her country about how the training could add value to people.

Builders are passionate about what they are doing and where they are going. And their passion inspires others to join them. Their can-do spirit spreads. Is there not enough time? They will find the time. Is there not enough money? They will find the money. Are there not enough people? They will find the people. How do they do it? By inspiring others to join and help them.

The bottom line for builders is that they always *build* something. They don't just talk about it. They are accomplished, and their track record is a great indicator of their future performance—and it qualifies them to try to lead others successfully.

Picking the right people to develop as leaders is so important. Red Auerbach, who was the longtime president of the NBA's Boston Celtics, said, "How you select people is more important than how you manage them once they're on the job. If you start with the right people, you won't have problems later on. If you hire the wrong people, for whatever reason, you're in serious trouble and all the revolutionary management techniques in the world won't bail you out."[15] The only way to have a great team is to identify and find the right people to develop as leaders.

Will they follow you and accept your input into their lives? That depends on your leadership. The Law of Buy-In from *The 21 Irrefutable*

Laws of Leadership says, "People buy in to the leader and then the vision."[16] And the Law of Respect in *The 21 Irrefutable Laws of Leadership* says, "People naturally follow leaders stronger than themselves."[17] That means people won't follow you if they are better leaders than you are. If your leadership ability is a 5 (out of 10), then you cannot expect people with a leadership ability of 6 or higher to follow you. You will have to keep working to become a better leader if you want to lead and develop people of higher caliber.

As much as I advocate identifying leaders in your own organization, sometimes you can't find who you're looking for there and you *must* look outside. But bringing in outsiders can create its own challenges because of the unknowns. I think the greatest unknown is cultural compatibility. I read an article in *Inc.* magazine by David Walker, CEO and cofounder of Triplemint real estate brokerage in New York City.[18] In it, Walker gave advice about hiring. He said, "If there's one thing that keeps every founder up at night, it's hiring. Hiring the best talent is a massive and never-ending challenge. . . . While every company has a different culture, there are four questions that will help you identify if a candidate is a good culture fit, no matter where your company falls on the culture spectrum."

Here are his four questions:

1. How did the culture at your last company empower or disempower you?
2. What were the characteristics of the best boss you've ever had?
3. Describe how you handled a conflict with one of your coworkers.
4. What kind of feedback do you expect to receive in this role and how often do you expect to receive it?

Here's what I love about Walker's approach. Asking the first question helps you understand the culture of your candidates' previous employers. Asking the second question helps you understand their view of leadership. Asking the third question helps you understand their relational skills. And asking the fourth question helps you understand their expectations regarding feedback.

Walker said, "I've made great hires who were a near-perfect culture fit, and I've made less-than-stellar hires who ultimately didn't work out. There is no such thing as batting a thousand with hiring. You're going to make mistakes no matter how good you are at it."

If you must bring outsiders into your organization, I think it's important to set expectations up front. In my book *Leadershift*, I wrote about the expectations we set for people when they join our team. We tell them:

- "It's not about me—it's not about you—it's about the big picture."
- "You are expected to keep growing."
- "You must value other people."
- "Always take responsibility."
- "We will not avoid tough conversations."[19]

The more we're on the same page, the better chance we all have of success.

If you want to lead a successful team or organization, you need to pick the right people to develop as leaders. Every person you bring onto your team or choose to develop will make you either better or worse. Peter Drucker observed:

Making the right people decisions is the ultimate means of controlling an organization well. Such decisions reveal how competent management is, what its values are, and whether it takes its job seriously. No matter how hard managers try to keep their decisions a secret—and some still try hard—people decisions cannot be hidden. They are eminently visible. . . .

Executives who do not make the effort to get their people decisions right do more than risk poor performance. They risk losing their organization's respect.[20]

If you get to know your team members, train them well, and observe them carefully, you greatly increase your chances of making good people decisions. You can choose the right people to develop as leaders. And just as you need to know what you're looking for in a potential leader, you need to know your goal for development. That's the subject of the next chapter.

ACTION STEPS

1. Spend time with each of your team members to familiarize or refamiliarize yourself with their personality, capabilities, working habits, and track record.

---

2. Plan to evaluate every member of your team. Give each person two scores for each of the characteristics listed in the chapter on a scale of one to ten (with ten as the highest score). The first score is an assessment of their current ability. The second is for what you believe to be their upside potential.

Name	Attitude	Character	Ability	Productivity	Improvement

3. Who stands out? Who has the highest starting scores? Who has the greatest upside potential? Both of those types can be developed as

leaders. Select the best of who you have, and plan to invite them into a leadership development process.

---

4. If your assessment is that not a single person on your team has leadership potential, before taking action to hire outsiders, ask the opinion of a trusted leader who knows your team whether they see anyone with potential. It's possible you're missing potential that is there. If other leaders agree with you, it might be time to recruit new team members with potential. If you do that, you will need to get to know them and equip them before beginning to develop them as leaders.

SIX

INVITE PEOPLE WITH POTENTIAL TO THE LEADERSHIP TABLE

I've always loved words and playing word games. Maybe that's because I've been a communicator and writer for more than forty years. One of my favorite words is *table*. It's a simple word, but it has a lot of positive connotations to me. The reason? Many of the richest experiences I have enjoyed in my life occurred around a table. That started in my childhood when my parents, brother, sister, and I ate dinner around the table at home. That was always a gathering place of joy in my life. And as I've gotten older, tables have been places where transformation occurs for myself and others.

Take, for example, the *meal table*. That can be used as a great *community of learning*. There is nothing I enjoy more than good food and good conversation—and believe me: I desire both. I love choosing a good restaurant, inviting people to join me around the table, and then asking them questions to create in-depth conversation. It can be magical. When it is, I find out a lot about the people around the table, and I learn new things that improve my life.

Another example is a *roundtable*. That can create a *community of helping*. The two nonprofit organizations I founded focus on being catalysts of transformation for communities and countries. Our efforts are accomplished by teaching values and leadership to people in roundtables—where small groups of men and women come together and discuss their experiences, apply values-based lessons to their lives, and hold one another accountable for positive change.

My favorite is the *leadership table* because it can be a *community of growth* for future leaders. Obviously in this case, the leadership table doesn't have to be a literal table. Having a leadership table means creating a place in your organization or on your team where people can learn, practice leadership with its successes and failures, and receive opportunities to shine.

Having a leadership table with open seats is perhaps the best way to start leaders in a development process and attract new leaders, not only within an organization, but also from outside. Why do I say that? Because nothing is more attractive to a potential leader than to be asked to sit at the leadership table.

The Law of Magnetism in my book *The 21 Irrefutable Laws of Leadership* states that who you are is who you attract.[1] People with leadership potential want to spend time with other leaders. They want to observe good leadership. They want to talk about it. They want to experience it. It fires them up. A true leadership table is a place where anyone with potential, the desire to lead, and the willingness to learn can sit and become part of your leadership team.

AN INVITATION TO THE TABLE

I remember an early experience where I was invited to a leadership table. It was in 1981, soon after I moved to San Diego. I was in my early thirties, and I had been leading in organizations for about a decade, but my experience was fairly limited. I received an invitation to attend a conference of leaders in Los Angeles. I felt as if I was being called up to the major leagues, because many of the leaders I respected were going to be at that meeting.

I can still remember feeling that I would be out of my league because the other leaders who had been invited were so much more experienced and successful than I was. Every doubt I had about myself intensified. Would I fit in? Would they accept me? Would I be able to contribute anything?

The day of the meeting, I walked into the room, and my fears disappeared immediately. What happened? Chuck Swindoll, who was the most influential leader in the group and someone I had admired for years, spotted me and came right over to me.

"John, we're so glad you came. Come sit with us," he said, walking me over to his table. "Here. Sit next to me so I can introduce you to the other leaders."

Being invited to that leadership table was huge for me, because it was the first time I remember being invited to join a group of high-level leaders I could learn from. It really opened my eyes to greater possibilities for my leadership.

No matter what level you occupy in leadership, you can create a leadership table, a place where people not yet leading at your level can come, be welcomed, and try on leadership. However, a leadership table shouldn't be an elite invitation to exclusivity; it should be an open invitation to opportunity. Anyone with leadership potential can be given a chance. We can often be surprised by who is able to rise up and lead effectively.

In his book *Too Many Bosses, Too Few Leaders*, business leadership and strategy consultant Rajeev Peshawaria, who is CEO of the Iclif Leadership and Governance Centre, said:

> The question is, in today's rapidly changing world, does it still make sense to identify a few, anoint them as high potentials, and invest disproportionately in their development?
>
> What if the world changes in ways that require a totally different type of potential in five years compared with the benchmarks used to identify today's high potentials? What about late bloomers—those who may not show early brilliance, but might become very valuable later on? And what about the negative impact on the morale of those not chosen as high potentials?
>
> For all of those reasons, it might be time to rethink the "best practice" of identifying and developing a pool of high potentials. Given the uncertainties of business today and the powerful forces shaping our lives . . . it is impossible to tell who will be the thought leaders of tomorrow. Instead of putting all their eggs in one basket of early-anointed high potentials, companies should expand their chances of producing future leaders by giving everyone a similar development diet and letting the cream rise to the top on its own.[2]

The table is meant to attract potential leaders and find out if they will become leaders.

Not everyone invited to the table will become an effective leader. And inviting someone to the leadership table does not mean that he or she will always remain there. The table is meant to attract potential leaders and find out if they will become leaders. For that reason, you should make the table as large as you can manage so that it will accommodate many potential players. And don't worry: the best leaders will separate themselves from the rest.

WHAT HAPPENS AT THE LEADERSHIP TABLE

To begin developing your potential leaders—and to make your team or organization attractive to other potential leaders—here's what you need to make sure happens at your leadership table:

1. EXPOSE THEM TO THE CULTURE OF A LEADERSHIP ENVIRONMENT

Leadership environments possess a leadership culture, because leaders think and act like leaders. They keep their eye on the big picture as well as the details. They think about the people as well as the processes. They weigh the intangibles, such as morale and momentum, as well as the bottom line. As I teach in the Law of Intuition in *The 21 Irrefutable Laws of Leadership*, leaders evaluate everything with a leadership bias. The way leaders work can at first feel alien to people who have never experienced that environment before.

In an article in *Harvard Business Review*, Bryan Walker and Sarah A. Soule said, "Culture is like the wind. It is invisible, yet its effect can be seen and felt. When it is blowing in your direction, it makes for smooth sailing. When it is blowing against you, everything is more difficult."[3] If you desire to develop leaders, you need to have the wind blowing with you, not against you. That means you must introduce leaders you want to develop to that leadership culture.

My friend Tim Elmore, founder and president of Growing Leaders, has written about culture in the workplace. He said:

You realize that the better the organizational culture, the less policies and corporate processes are required to enforce behavior. When the culture is strong, it's like the tide that raises all the boats on the water. Think about organizations that seem to get this:

- Zappos
- Starbucks
- Chick-fil-A
- Netflix

This works in reverse, as well. The weaker the culture, the more leaders must rely on policies and procedures to make people behave in a certain way. *What you lack in culture, you must make up for in legislation.* Colin Angle, cofounder of iRobot said it this way: "Culture is the magic start-up ingredient."[4]

What Tim described in particular is a *leadership* culture. Organizations with a strong leadership culture depend on *people* for guidance and direction, not rules and policies.

The foundation of the leadership culture in my organizations is created by good values. We want the people we develop to have our values. We want them to value people and add value to people. People who lacks those values won't fit in our environment and won't be able to develop as leaders.

One of the organizations I greatly admire is Chick-fil-A. It has an outstanding culture, and people line up not only for the food, but for jobs as operators and employees. Mack Story, a successful Maxwell Leadership Certified Team member, wrote of Chick-fil-A (CFA):

How would you like to be able to select the "right" person from 250 applications when you fill a position? Would you be more likely to have a better, stronger team when picking from a handful of applicants or 250? There's a reason CFA has this many applicants. It's because of who they are.

Anyone with money can buy the same equipment and build the same type of building in the same great location. And, many do. But, they don't get the same results. Why? Because most are not in the people development business. They are in the fast food business. CFA develops people that serve other people. Therefore, they attract people that value developing and serving other people. Sure, they have the privilege of turning away a lot of people that do not qualify, but they get to pick those that share their values.

It's been my observation that many organizations are in the "profit" business. They operate much differently than those in the people development business. Ironically, those in the people development business tend to make a lot more profit because, in the end, the people are responsible for the profit.[5]

A company's environment is the expression of the values of the people within the organization. It is the sum of the behavior of the people, not a reflection of what you want it to be. People do what people see—and they keep doing it. What people do on an ongoing, habitual basis creates culture.

> A company's culture is the expression of the values of the people within the organization.

When leaders gather together, talk about leadership, and practice good leadership together, it creates a leadership environment. When they continue to do those things over time, it creates a leadership culture. When you invite one or more potential leaders to that leadership "table," they receive the opportunity to learn and grow by understanding how leaders think, what they value, and how they work. When potential leaders begin to adopt those same methods, their leadership development process has begun.

2. ENCOURAGE THEM TO PARTICIPATE IN THE DYNAMICS OF THE TABLE

If you don't have a group of established leaders who make up a leadership table, then you will need to create a developmental table yourself. Creating a leadership table allows you to provide a good environment for your team members to grow, learn, and begin embracing the dynamics of leadership. It can be a fantastic tool for shaping leaders, but you must become intentional about taking people through a growth process.

I've had the pleasure of vacationing several times in Florence, Italy, and every time I visit, I make sure to go to the Accademia Gallery to see Michelangelo's *David*. When questioned about his masterpiece, Michelangelo is alleged to have said that the sculpture already existed within the stone; he simply had to chisel away the rock around it.[6]

That's what leaders do. They see the future leader within the person, and they help that leader emerge. Maybe that's why professor and bestselling author Brené Brown defined a leader as "anyone who takes responsibility for finding the potential in people . . . and who has the courage to develop that potential."[7]

In the last several years, my organizations have discovered the power of roundtables for promoting personal growth as well as leadership development in people. The dynamics of small group gatherings where everyone is asked to participate can be powerful. People discover new ideas, have their thinking challenged, are prompted to apply what they learn, and hold each other accountable for making positive change in their lives. My nonprofit organizations have trained tens of thousands of leaders internationally in how to host values roundtables. Those leaders have helped hundreds of thousands of people grow in character, leadership, and intentional living. The positive impact on people's lives has been profound.

Our Maxwell Leadership Certified Team members also receive intentional leadership training with my book *Developing the Leader Within You 2.0.* They participate in a leadership roundtable where they read and discuss chapters, challenge one another to grow, and hold each other accountable. And because they are being encouraged to start or improve their coaching and speaking businesses at the same time, they have opportunities to apply what they learn in a real-life context.

As you invite people to a leadership table, be sure to do the following:

Set Up-Front Expectations with Invitees

The first thing you need to do when you invite potential leaders to the table is establish expectations. Here's what you need to tell them:

- The format of the group is honest discussion.
- The environment is one of encouragement.
- Everyone in the group must participate.
- There are no bad questions.
- Everyone's aim should be to add value to what's shared.
- The purpose of the roundtable is application, not information.
- Everyone is held accountable for following through with commitments.

Lose Yourself and Focus on Your People

As the leader of a roundtable, you are not to teach anything. Your goal is to ask questions and facilitate discussion. Be open and authentic about yourself and your journey, but focus on others, giving them 100 percent of your attention. Place a high value on everyone, and whenever possible, validate what they say.

Expect Them to Add Value to the Table

Adding value is what leaders do for others. As the leader of a group, you need to model it by doing your best to add value to people at the table, and you should encourage it from others. Whenever possible, allow people to team up to share with one another what has been most helpful to them. This increases learning and gives people experience adding value to others.

Encourage Everyone to ACT

Knowledge isn't the key to success. Applying knowledge is. That's how we grow. And for that reason, action must always be the goal when leaders and potential leaders gather together.

For many years, I've taught something I call ACT, which stands for *apply, change, teach.* Anytime I am in a growth setting, whether it's a roundtable, a conference, or a meeting, I listen for things I can ACT upon. I encourage you to use this and to help people in your group. At the end of every session, ask people, based on what was discussed:

- "What can you *apply* to your life?"
- "What can you *change* about yourself?"
- "What can you *teach* to someone else to help them?"

Then at the beginning of the next session, ask individuals what they committed to ACT upon in the previous session and to share how they followed through. You'll be amazed at how quickly people begin applying what they learn when they know others will ask about it and hold them accountable.

Watch the Eyes at the Table

One of the greatest benefits of facilitating a leadership roundtable is that you see potential leaders rise at the table. You learn how people think and solve problems. You observe how they communicate with others. You learn about their character and follow-through. And you see how others respond to them. The people who see more and before others in the group start to emerge as leaders. Others intuitively sense it and respect them. When you ask questions, you'll begin to see their influence because others will start looking at them for answers. The best leaders separate themselves from everyone else. Pay attention to them and tag them for more personalized development later on.

3. ALLOW THEM TO BENEFIT FROM THE POWER OF PROXIMITY

There was a time in history when most people learned a trade or profession by apprenticing under a master craftsman. The apprentice would follow the craftsman everywhere, observing his work, assisting him, asking questions after learning the basics, and eventually practicing the craft under his watchful eye. But how does the learning process usually happen today? People attend lectures in a classroom, watch videos, or read books. As someone who writes books and teaches to audiences, I value these processes, but they're not the same as a close, hands-on experience with leaders "at the table."

I recently saw some interesting statistics about how people learn:

- Learners that will transfer a new skill into their practice as a result of learning a theory = 5%

- Learners that will transfer a new skill into their practice as a result of learning a theory and seeing a demonstration = 10%
- Learners that will transfer a new skill into their practice as a result of theory, demonstration and practice during the training = 20%
- Learners that will transfer a new skill into their practice as a result of theory, demonstration, practice and corrective feedback during the training = 25%
- Learners that will transfer a new skill into their practice as a result of theory, demonstration, practice, feedback during training and in-situation coaching or mentoring = 90%[8]

As a learner, there's no substitute for participating and having access to people who know what they're doing, can direct you, and can give you feedback. That requires proximity.

Leadership is more caught than taught. That's why one of the best ways for potential leaders to learn how leaders think, problem-solve, and act is to spend time with them at the table. Getting the opportunity to be present in a strategy meeting is eye-opening. Listening to leaders wrestle through issues, seeing how they make choices, and watching how they interact with one another are some of the best gifts a potential leader can receive from you. Meeting rooms can be classrooms for potential leaders.

> Leadership is more caught than taught.

Of course, there are other intentional ways to bring leaders and potential leaders together to learn from one another. For example, every year I host a Maxwell Leadership event where we take 120 leaders to a different city for a leadership experience. This event, called Exchange, is highly desired and always sells out. Why? The proximity of leaders to one another. For three days leaders from a variety of businesses and with diverse backgrounds come together to discuss leadership and experience growth. It's like leadership show-and-tell on steroids. Many of the attendees forge lifetime friendships at Exchange and are impacted by lessons that change the course of their lives.

Another way I help leaders develop at the table is to participate in phone calls with different groups of leaders every month to teach, answer questions, and promote discussion. Technology allows me to develop a kind of proximity to people around the world and convey the spirit of leadership to everyone who was on the call. If you need to use technology to gather together a table of leaders, then use it. Do whatever you can to create a leadership environment where potential leaders can learn.

4. Let Them Practice Leadership

In the end, the only way for any person to learn leadership is to lead. Leading isn't a theoretical exercise. *Lead* is a verb, and to get better at leadership, people must start leading, whether they're leading as a businessperson, a volunteer, an employee, a parent, or a coach. Everybody has to start somewhere. Why not let your potential leaders start practicing at the table with you and other leaders who can help them?

> The only way for any person to learn leadership is to lead. Leading isn't a theoretical exercise.

In his book *Bounce*, Matthew Syed wrote about the power of practice over talent. He cited a study performed in 1991 by psychologist Anders Ericsson and two colleagues. They studied violinists at the Music Academy of West Berlin. They divided the children into three groups based on their perceived level of ability:

- Students capable of careers as international star soloists
- Students capable of careers in the world's best orchestras
- Students capable of careers teaching music

These ratings were based on the opinions of the school professors and the students' performances in open competitions.

What Ericsson discovered was that biographies of the students in all three groups were remarkably similar. Most began practice at age eight, decided to become musicians right before they turned fifteen, had usually studied under four teachers, and had on average studied 1.8 other instruments in addition to the violin. There was no remarkable difference in talent between them when they started. So, what was the difference? Practice time! By age twenty, the bottom group had practiced four thousand fewer hours than the middle group, and the middle group had practiced two thousand fewer hours than the top group, which had practiced ten thousand hours. "There were no exceptions to this pattern," said Syed of Ericsson's findings. "Purposeful practice was the only factor distinguishing the best from the rest."[9]

If you want to develop leaders, you need to encourage them to begin practicing their leadership and giving them a place to do it. The leadership table is the place to start.

My mother used to tell me that birds of a feather flock together. If you want to improve yourself, find a flock that's better than you are at leadership, and join their flock. If you want to develop potential leaders, put them in groups with people smarter, more experienced, and better than they are. It's good to remember that if someone is always at the head of the class, he or she is in the wrong class. If their potential is high, they will rise to the occasion. They will start to become the leaders you need to make your team and organization better.

> If someone is always at the head of the class, he or she is in the wrong class.

ACTION STEPS

1. Do you have experience having been invited to or included in a leadership table? When have you been around a group of leaders from whom you were able to learn? If you *have not* experienced it, how has that slowed down your development as a leader? What have you had to learn the hard way that other leaders might have taught you? If you *have* experienced it, list all the ways you benefited.

   _____

2. If you can identify an existing leadership group where you can include leaders you want to develop, then gain permission from the leaders in the group to bring one or more of the leaders you desire to develop. Establish whether those developing leaders are welcome to participate at the table or whether they are allowed to contribute. Then communicate those ground rules to the people you invite.

   _____

3. Create your own leadership roundtable where potential leaders are expected to learn, grow, and participate. Develop your strategy for how they will learn. Will you ask them to read books? Will you take them to leadership events? Will you take them through classes together? Will you discuss the work you're doing together from a leadership angle? Determine how it will work, then invite them to the table. Then establish expectations with them up front.

   _____

4. Start letting people lead. Give the potential leaders you're developing changes to stretch their leadership legs. Over time, you will
start to see who the better thinkers are at the table and who the
better practitioners are away from the table. Value and develop both
types.

SEVEN

KNOW THE GOAL OF
DEVELOPING YOUR LEADERS

Before we go any further, it's important to discuss your goal as a developer of leaders. Once you've invited people with potential to the leadership table and begin working with them, what do you want them to become? Obviously, every organization is unique, and so are the goals and work that must be done. And different kinds of leaders need different skills to be successful in their areas. But are there key areas where *all* leaders can develop?

3-G LEADERSHIP

The answer is yes. When I develop leaders, I want to be certain they are developed in three core areas, which I think of as the three Gs. Good leaders are *grounded*, *gifted*, and *growing*. No matter who they lead or what kind of job they're responsible for, the three Gs create a solid foundation upon which to further develop their leadership skills.

Let's take a look at each of them.

1. Grounded—Possessing Core Values That Make Them Solid

Like begets like. That's a universal law. I look for leaders who have a solid foundation, who are grounded. What do I mean by that? Here are the characteristics I seek in a grounded leader:

Integrity

The most important value of a leader is integrity. Without it, leaders are destined to self-destruct and take others with them. My friend Pat Williams, senior vice president of the Orlando Magic, said, "One of the primary rules of navigation is this: What's under the surface should carry more weight than what's above the surface if the ship is going to make it through storms without capsizing. That's exactly how it is with integrity. What's under the surface had better be greater than what you're showing to the world, or you're never going to make it through the storms of life."

I think of having integrity as being bigger on the inside than we are on the outside. Leaders with integrity have the strength to take others through storms without capsizing. As you work with new leaders, confirm and affirm their integrity. Challenge them to do the right things, even when they're difficult, and praise them when they follow through. And if you see any cracks in a leader's integrity, address them immediately. Your leaders need to know what the standard is and be given a chance to meet it. But if they don't, they must be removed from leadership.

Authenticity

Authenticity is the new authority in leadership, not power or position. Authentic people are aware of their strengths and weaknesses and don't try to be what they're not. The leaders you develop need to be realistic about who they are, demonstrating that they're neither overly impressed with themselves nor depressed about themselves. They must become comfortable in their own skin. Even if their ability is off the charts, they need to think like former South Africa president Nelson Mandela, who said, "I do not want to be presented as some deity. I would like to be remembered as an ordinary human being with virtues and vices."[1]

If you want to develop leaders with authenticity, they you need to model authenticity. You need to be honest about your shortcomings as well as your strengths. You need to be your same authentic self with your boss, your colleagues, and your team members. If you value and demonstrate authenticity as well as holding your leaders to that same standard, they will begin to value it too.

Humility

My mentor John Wooden was the humblest leader I have ever known. One of the things he used to say was, "Talent is God-given; be humble. Fame is man-given; be thankful. Conceit is self-given; be careful."[2] Those are great words of warning for leaders.

Teachability

Talented leaders are often strong-willed and confident. Those are good qualities. However, talent can also make people hardheaded. It's difficult to teach someone who isn't open to change, who has little desire to learn. You can't afford to waste time trying to develop someone who won't learn or improve.

As you develop potential leaders, be on the lookout for signs of resistance to teachability. I've found the development of teachability comes in stages, and you can look for where a new leader is on that spectrum. Take a look at them:

1. They don't seek advice.
2. They don't want advice.
3. They don't object to advice.
4. They do listen to advice.
5. They do welcome advice.
6. They do actively seek advice.
7. They do follow the advice given to them.
8. They do give others credit for their advice.

When you look at the new leaders you're developing, where are they? Ideally, you'd like to get all of them to stage eight. But if you can't get them to at least stage three, where they don't object to advice, you should probably stop trying to develop them.

The best way thing to do with leaders who aren't very teachable is to talk to them directly about it. Point out the specific instances in which they displayed lack of teachability, explain how open to learning they need to become to be developed by you, and ask them to change, letting them know you will hold them accountable.

Maturity

Many years ago, columnist Ann Landers wrote a marvelous piece on maturity, where she described it as patience, perseverance, self-control, integrity, responsibility, and dependability. It's the ability to say, "I was wrong," to keep a promise, to make decisions, and to follow through. She finished by writing a variation on the Serenity Prayer: "Maturity is the art of living in peace with that which we cannot change, the courage to change that which should be changed, no matter what it takes, and the wisdom to know the difference."[3]

These are qualities that can be developed, regardless of age. I've met many young people who possessed maturity early in life. And I've known plenty of older people who lack these qualities. Model, value, and reward this kind of maturity to cultivate it in your leaders.

Integrity, authenticity, humility, teachability, and maturity provide a solidly grounded foundation upon which to build strong leadership. When leadership development focuses too much on the how-tos of leadership and not enough on the solid core of who the person is, the results can be shallow and short-lived. By working with grounded people—and strengthening that groundedness—you can go deep and develop leaders whose inner lives are solid and strong no matter what they face. And that's important. I once heard retired NFL coach Tony Dungy say, "When you are playing to win, are you going to place anyone in a position that you can't totally count on? The answer is no." When leaders are grounded, you can depend on them.

2. GIFTED—USING THEIR STRENGTHS TO LEAD WELL

There is no substitute for a lack of giftedness. Ability determines potential. The giftedness of leaders is the first step making it possible for them to grow and succeed. There's an old saying among coaches: you can't put in what God has left out. Or as my legendary coaching friend, Lou Holtz, put it in a quip he once made over lunch, "I've coached good players and I've coached bad players. I'm a better coach with better players." I think that's true for any leader. The more talented and gifted the leaders on the team, the more successful the team has the potential to be.

Good leaders lean into their giftedness. They use their strengths to lead well. And the people who develop them know that. When it comes to talent, never focus on developing weaknesses. Always focus on developing strengths.

Why is focusing on giftedness so important?

Giftedness Gives an Advantage—Don't Let Them Abuse It

Gifted leaders see more than and before others see. They spot problems when they're on the distant horizon. They see solutions before they're evident to others. Their instincts often inform their decision-making. All these things give them a distinct advantage.

> Every day, every leader you work with should ask, "Am I using my gifts for myself or others?"

As you develop gifted leaders, you need to help them understand that they should use their gifts to advance the team and organization, not use them for personal gain. Every day, every leader you work with should ask, "Am I using my gifts for myself or others?" If they don't already think that way, you need to teach it to them.

Giftedness Gives Opportunity—Don't Let Them Miss It

In his book *Aspire*, Kevin Hall wrote: "I believe that effective people are not problem-minded; they're opportunity-minded. The root of opportunity is *port*, meaning the entryway by water into a city or place of business. In earlier days, when the tide and winds were right, and the port opened, it allowed entry to do commerce, to visit, or to invade and conquer. But only those who recognized the opening could take advantage of the open port, or opportunity."[4]

When you develop leaders, you need to prepare them today to seize opportunities in the future based on their giftedness. That's important because no one should wait to start preparing until the opportunity arrives. By then it's too late. When we get an opportunity, we need to jump on it. Get them ready by helping them leverage their strengths to advance the team.

Giftedness Requires Humility—Model It and Expect It of Them

Have you ever received a fantastic gift out of the blue from someone who loves you? Maybe a birthday or Christmas from your childhood stands out in your memory because of what you received from your mother or father. Maybe a sibling or close friend blessed you with a great gift. Or maybe your spouse gave you something extraordinary for an anniversary or other special occasion. How did it make you feel? Grateful? Excited? Humbled?

When you receive a gift, you should never take credit for receiving it—because it was a *gift*. Whatever natural talents and abilities we were born with cannot be credited to us. We didn't do anything to earn them. We don't deserve them. We should be grateful. We should make the most of them. But remembering that they were *gifts* keeps us humble.

As my mentor consultant Fred Smith said, "The gift is greater than the person." He was teaching me that the successes I experience as a result of my gifting are greater than I am as a person. They exceed my ability. He was saying that as a person of faith, I should gratefully acknowledge God as the giver of my giftedness; he is done for me so many things I cannot do for myself.

As a leader, maintain perspective and model humility. And help the leaders you develop to gain perspective if they lose it. Their giftedness opens the door for them. Their hard work will keep the door open. And the reason they should go through that door is to serve others, not themselves.

Giftedness Requires Responsibility—Help Them Accept It

When I was growing up, my father often told me, "To whomsoever much is given, of him shall much be required."[5] That sense of responsibility for making the most of my giftedness became a part of me. Scientist and teacher George Washington Carver said in 1915, "No individual has any right to come into the world and go out of it without leaving behind him distinct and legitimate reasons for having passed through it."[6] That sets a high standard for anyone, but I believe the standard for leaders is even higher, because they often have greater gifts and have the potential to make a greater impact.

Encourage your leaders to take responsibility for making the most of their gifts and using them to make a difference, not only for your team and organization, but beyond. Good leaders can leave the world better than they find it. The more they harness their gifts for good, the greater the positive impact they can make.

3. Growing—Possessing a Hunger and Capacity to Keep Learning and Developing

The final G has to do with growth. What is a good sign that a leader has the hunger and capacity to be developed? He is already growing. Because we're discussing developing leaders, a pattern of growth is essential. Ideally, the leaders you are developing will already be growing and understand the growth process. If not, you will need to help them get there.

The most important growth area you need to help leaders work on is how they think. That is what separates successful from unsuccessful people. There's a gap between the way those two kinds of people think. As you develop them, challenge their thinking in these areas:

Help Them to Think Better

Leaders can never afford to sit back and let someone else do their thinking for them. Good leaders are proactive. They entertain new ideas and new methods of doing things. They consider intangibles, such as culture, morale, timing, and momentum. They drill down to details, but they always keep the big picture in mind. They size up situations quickly and make decisions based on the information they have, along with what their instincts tell them. All of these actions require good thinking.

When you begin developing leaders, the most important thing you can do is help them develop their thinking ability. Start by letting them know what you're thinking and why. I've already suggested that you bring them to the table and let them in on meetings and discussions so that they can learn how you and other top leaders think. The more exposure they get to good thinkers and the more practice they get applying what they learn, the better their thinking will become.

> When you begin developing leaders, the most important thing you can do is let them know what you're thinking and why.

Encourage Them to Think Bigger

Most people think too small. Good leaders can't afford to do that. They need to think expansively for the sake of the vision and the team. As writer and coach David J. Schwartz said, "Where success is concerned, people are not measured in inches, or pounds, or college degrees, or family background; they are measured by the size of their thinking. How big we think determines the size of our accomplishments."[7]

Help the leaders you develop to expand their thinking. Challenge them. Ask them to stretch their aspiration. People usually rise to the level of expectations of a leader who believes in them. Show your new leaders how much you believe in them, and push them to invest their belief in those they are leading. When it comes to belief, a rising tide lifts all boats.

Ask Them to Think with Creativity

The best leaders I know think outside of the box. They don't simply color within the lines. They redraw the picture. They seek options. They not only believe there is a solution to every problem; they believe there are multiple solutions, and they work to find the best ones.

As you develop leaders, help them to cultivate their creative thinking ability. Encourage them to push the boundaries of what's possible. Prompt them to look at old problems in new ways. And ask them to be open and harness creativity within the teams they lead so they can be innovative and effective.

Expect Them to Think About People

As leadership responsibility increases, so does pressure. Under stressful circumstances, some leaders start to forget how important people are. They focus instead on results and systems. They make everything about the bottom line. But leadership is *always* about people. If people aren't involved, then what you're doing is no longer leadership. And if what you're doing isn't benefiting people, you've lost your way as a leader.

No matter how high a leader climbs, no matter how heavy their responsibilities become, no matter how big their organization gets, no matter how much success they achieve, people always matter. Good leaders continuously think about people first and how to add value to them. As you develop leaders, make sure they embrace that belief and practice it continually.

A LEADER AT THE TABLE SETTING TABLES FOR OTHERS

My greatest joy as a leader has been developing other leaders. Today, at age seventy-five, I am still as excited about it as I've ever been. One of the leaders I invited to my leadership table twenty years ago is John Vereecken.

I first met John back in 2000, when he was thirty-five. He is originally from Michigan, but he and his wife, Karla, have lived and worked in Mexico since 1985. It didn't take John long to realize the leadership culture of Latin America was very different from what he grew up with in the United States. While people the US have a can-do attitude and believe they can accomplish anything, the people of Latin America tended to be more tentative. And those who did want to lead did so by working to attain positions of power where they could tell others what to do. John wanted to try to change that. He dreamed of helping people in Mexico and the rest of Latin America to embrace a model of leadership where leaders add value to people, encourage and empower them, and help them grow and succeed.

John said he had read *The 21 Irrefutable Laws of Leadership* and *The 17 Indisputable Laws of Teamwork*, and those books had made him realize he could become a better leader, and anyone can learn to lead. Just by talking with John, I could see such great potential in him. He was already doing a lot, and I wanted to help him. So, I said, "You have my permission to take those two books, translate them into Spanish, and teach them anywhere you want in Latin America." I also offered to teach leadership to him and his best leaders once a year.

John later confessed that when I said he could use my materials to teach leadership, he thought, *He thinks we can do this?* He didn't know what he was capable of, but he was willing. Not long after that, he was teaching the 21 Laws in San Pedro Sula, Honduras, and he began to see the light bulbs turn on for people from businesses, government, education, and churches. They realized that leadership wasn't position and power. It was influence, and it could be used to help people.

I watched as John successfully trained leaders all over Latin America, and I spent more time with him, giving him advice and developing him. And when my nonprofit organization EQUIP was ready to start training leaders in Central and South America, you know who I called on to help me: John. His organization, Lidere, facilitated the leadership training of half a million people with EQUIP. And I continue to work with him. He's been a vital contributor to the John Maxwell Foundation's initiatives in Guatemala, Paraguay, and Costa Rica. Today, John oversees the leadership transformation projects of my nonprofit organizations in all of Latin America.

I asked John to tell me his perspective on our interaction, and here's what he had to say:

> You believed in me when I didn't even know what leadership was. I thought, *He knows what he's doing, and if he thinks I can, then I guess I can. I don't want to let him down.*
>
> You developed me in so many ways. You loaned me your platform, which opened doors of opportunity that I never would have had. You invested in me through mentoring phone calls, at dinners, on plane flights, and backstage before events. You answered questions, and shared leadership wisdom and practices. You gave me opportunities to lead. Being given the opportunity to lead several large initiatives in Latin America forced me to lift my leadership lid. Having the opportunity to translate for you when you speak with a country's president or to an audience on stage has been *the* greatest opportunity of accelerated development in my life. And just the opportunity to interact with people and work in a leadership culture of your companies has provided me with opportunities to grow in areas of my leadership and people skills.

What John Vereecken described is being invited to the leadership table and being developed. I don't want you to miss this. John came to the table with his skills and aspirations. He wanted and needed help. He experienced the dynamics of the table. He benefited from proximity—even though he lived in Mexico and we only met in person occasionally. And he received opportunities to lead—which he *ran* with. He was excellent. He is a true 3-G leader.

You can do the same thing with people. You can start developing leaders where you are. You just need to know what the goal of leadership development is, what target you're shooting for.

Mark Miller, vice president of high performance leadership at Chick-fil-A, has vast experience finding and training leaders. He said:

> I'm wondering how often, as a leader, we fail to clearly define the target. I think about all the times my leadership efforts have fallen short . . . how many of those failures can be attributed, directly or indirectly, to an unclear target or goal?
>
> There are many things leaders CANNOT do for their people. However, clarity regarding intent should never be in short supply. People must always know what they are trying to accomplish.[8]

You can personally develop people in groundedness, gifting, and growth so that they become 3-G leaders. You don't need to be an expert to do it, nor do you need to be experienced. The first time I tried to develop someone, I was in my twenties, and though I did the best I could, I didn't do a very good job. But I didn't quit. I kept developing people. I started small and got better at it. I just kept inviting people to the leadership table and working with them to develop them. You can do the same.

ACTION STEPS

1. Tell all of the leaders that you are developing that you want to sit down with each of them individually to talk about their core values, and you want them to identify their values beforehand. When you meet, ask them to identify their values, why they chose them, and what they mean to them. Ask their permission to hold them accountable to those values. If their list does not include integrity, authenticity, humility, teachability, and maturity, explain why you regard those values highly and ask if they would be willing to be held accountable to those values too. If they refuse, let them know you will not be able to develop them as leaders. If they agree, then begin paying attention to whether they uphold their values, and work with them if they are falling short.

2. Identify the strengths and gifting of the leaders you're developing. Ask them to take assessments, such as Strengths Finder or Right Path if that would be helpful. Then sit down with each leader to discuss those strengths. See if they agree or have additional strengths you did not identify. Ask them to identify their weaknesses as well. If they are not self-aware, you may need to help them to develop that quality.

3. Develop a plan for allowing your leaders to take on tasks that appear to be in their strength zones, that rely on their giftedness. As they complete each task, discuss how it went. Together determine whether their performance supports what you believed to be their strengths and weaknesses or whether you need to do a reassessment.

4. Ask your leaders to read books and meet with them as a group to discuss them and apply the lessons they learn. In addition, challenge each of them to put themselves on personal growth plans that develop their strengths and help them to become better thinkers. Recommend and provide resources for books, podcasts, seminars, or courses.

EIGHT

EMPOWER NEW LEADERS TO LEAD

One of the most powerful things you can do as a leader is release the leaders you develop to reach their potential.

If you've read Gallup's statistics on employee disengagement, then you probably recognize that the majority of people working today are not close to reaching their potential. Why? Because they feel they're not in the right job, they're not using their strengths, and they're not excited about the work they do.[1] Empowering people can change that. And if those you empower are leaders, it has a multiplying effect, because every leader you empower can help empower the people they lead to reach their potential too.

Where does the ability to empower others come from? It is based primarily on earning respect, building relationships, and providing an environment of empowerment. If you've done everything discussed in the previous seven chapters, you've earned respect and developed leadership credibility. And you've built relationships with the people you've equipped and begun to develop. Now you need to create an environment of empowerment where you increasingly release your new leaders to lead.

EMPOWERMENT REQUIRES A SECURE LEADER

Before I show you what an empowering environment looks like, I need to tell you something about your relationship with the new leaders you intend to empower. If you want to maintain a long-term professional relationship with people and continually empower them, you must be respected and liked. If the people who work with you respect you but don't like you, they will stay with you only until they find a leader they respect *and* like. On the other hand, if they like you but don't respect you, they might be your friends, but they won't follow you. Developing both gives you the authority to empower.

> Only secure leaders give power to others.

The Law of Empowerment in *The 21 Irrefutable Laws of Leadership* states, "Only secure leaders give power to others."[2] As a leader, I can have one of two attitudes toward the people who work with me. I can try to impress them with what I can do, or I can empower them by helping them do what they can do. I cannot do both at the same time.

And you cannot empower people if you allow your insecurities to control you. Why? Insecure leaders want to be the center of everything. They love the incredible emotional return of feeling indispensable. They make everything all about themselves, and what they do is motivated by *preserving* their power, not giving it away. To become an empowering leader, you must use the power you have to help your leaders achieve their dreams.

In their book *It's Not About You*, authors Bob Burg and John David Mann shared news for insecure leaders:

> You are not their dreams, you are only the steward of those dreams. And leaders often get it backwards and start thinking they not only hold the best of others, but they are the best. . . . The moment you start thinking it's all about you, that *you're the deal*, is the moment you begin losing your capacity to positively influence others' lives.[3]

It's also the moment you lose your capacity to empower people to become better leaders.

Secure leaders who value people think of others first. They don't remove themselves from the big picture; they just take on a less obvious role. They help others become more prominent because they recognize that those "others" are the key to the success of the team or organization. Secure leaders also don't have to be the ones to win every time. They want others to win because they understand that's how the new leaders, the team and the organization win.

The greatest leaders aren't necessarily the ones who do the greatest things. They are the ones who empower *others* to do great things. To do that, leaders need to be willing to give up center stage. They must give up the need to be needed by others. Instead, they must cheer on the people they empower when they succeed, not feel threatened by their success. They must point to the victories of others and celebrate their successes. That's what secure, relational leaders do.

> The greatest leaders aren't necessarily the ones who do the greatest things. They are the ones who empower *others* to do great things.

HOW TO CREATE AN EMPOWERING ENVIRONMENT

As a leader, you can help people rise up, grow, and reach for their potential. If you function in an organization that values and promotes empowerment, you may find creating this kind of environment relatively easy, because it's already part of the culture. However, if your organization doesn't have that kind of positive culture, you can still work to create space for your leaders to rise up by promoting and facilitating empowerment on your team.

Take a look at the six characteristics of an empowering environment, make note of how many of them describe your organization or team, and think about ways you could promote them where you lead:

1. Empowering Environments Embrace Everyone's Potential

The main limitation most people have on their lives is their low expectations of themselves. Most people are unaware of the possibilities that lie within them. Good leaders create environments that introduce the people they lead to those wonderful possibilities. And the best people to start with are the leaders.

The first time I spoke at the Walmart headquarters in Bentonville, Arkansas, I read these words over the doorway as I entered into a large meeting room: "Through these doors pass ordinary people on their way to accomplishing extraordinary things." That's the kind of mind-set an empowering environment promotes.

One of the leaders I enjoy encouraging and empowering is Traci Morrow. She is a highly successful entrepreneur with Beachbody, has been a Maxwell Leadership Certified Team member for many years, and recently became one of our organization's growth plan guides. Traci recently sent me a note thanking me for empowering her. She wrote,

"You have always valued me, and I have witnessed firsthand what it feels like to be treated like you have put a 10 on my forehead (after hearing you teach people to do so for years). I may not always operate as a 10, but you have never treated me as less. That inspires me to rise, think, act, and grow toward that number. I feel both believed in and equipped to grow past my own lids. In turn, I want to do that for those I'm blessed to mentor."

Traci understands the releasing power of an empowering environment and endeavors to create that environment for the people she leads. While most good leaders focus on raising the bar of potential for themselves, empowering leaders also raise up their people. They want them to go above and beyond the jobs they perform. Their mind-set is opposite of the one expressed by Henry Ford, when he complained, "Why is it that I always get the whole person, when what I really want is a pair of hands?"[4]

Empowerment is so much bigger than training people's hands to do the work that needs to be done. It's about encouraging the whole person to rise up and be more. It's about helping new leaders see their potential, believing they can achieve it, and encouraging them to rise up to it.

2. Empowering Environments Give Team Members Freedom

For others to soar, they must first be free to fly. How do you help them have that freedom? By reducing unneeded rules and bureaucracy. Nordstrom stores became famous in the 1990s for giving their employees the freedom to help people. Their motto reportedly was: "Use your own good judgment in all situations. There will be no more rules." That's why Nordstrom's customer service was notoriously spectacular.

I once heard the saying "Before you remove a fence, first ask why it was placed there." All leaders desire to increase their territory. Are there "fences" around your leaders that might once have been help-ful but are now obstacles to their progress? What are they? Are there restrictions that you could eliminate? Are there programs that once worked but no longer do that you can eliminate? Are there procedures that the organization has outgrown that need to be abandoned? Are there policies that hold leaders back instead of empowering them to move forward? You need to be willing to bury a "dead" program, proce-dure, or policy that's holding your leaders back. As Peter Drucker said, "The corpse doesn't smell any better the longer you keep it around."[5]

Leaders who create an empowering environment give new leaders and team members the freedom to think for themselves, try things their way, and share their ideas. That's one of the best ways they develop leaders. An organization that values empowerment wants innovative leaders, not clones. Empowering leaders know that there are no limits to the future of the team if they don't put limits on their people.

3. Empowering Environments Encourage Collaboration

Empowering environments do more than promote cooperation, which can be described as working together agreeably. They encour-age collaboration, which is working together aggressively. One of the most collaborative environments I've ever read about is Pixar, the anima-tion studio run for many years by Ed Catmull. In his book *Creativity, Inc.*, he described how every part of Pixar was led with the idea of empowering people and encouraging collaboration. He described his way of thinking like

> "If we start with the attitude that different viewpoints are additive rather than competitive, we become more effective because our ideas or decisions are honed and tempered by that discourse."
>
> —ED CATMULL

this: "If we start with the attitude that different viewpoints are additive rather than competitive, we become more effective because our ideas or decisions are honed and tempered by that discourse."[6]

Encouraging collaboration among team members and new leaders reduces silos and turf wars. It promotes creativity and innovation, and builds a more positive and empowering environment. I'll discuss this in greater detail in chapter 10.

4. EMPOWERING ENVIRONMENTS PROMOTE ACCOUNTABILITY

Giving leaders the freedom to act but neglecting to make them accountable for their actions can create chaos. Authority and accountability always need to walk hand in hand. As leadership author Ken Blanchard wrote, "Empowerment means you have the freedom to act. It also means you are accountable for the results."[7]

When we give freedom to leaders, we need to let them know that they are accountable to produce results and to be consistent. Some people believe that credibility is earned after it has been demonstrated once. That's not true. Consistent competence must be renewed daily in everything we do. And new leaders need to acknowledge that they will never arrive at a place where they no longer need to be responsible to others. People always produce better results when they are held accountable.

5. EMPOWERING ENVIRONMENTS GIVE LEADERS OWNERSHIP

Responsibility in leadership is important. Holding people accountable prompts them to accept that responsibility. However, there is a higher level of commitment: ownership. When you empower your leaders to own a job, project, or task, they do everything in their power to bring it to completion. They are preoccupied with getting results. They get up in the morning and go to bed at night thinking about what they're responsible for. They go the extra mile without being asked. And they don't quit until the job is done. They feel the weight of ownership.

How do you measure this level of engagement in a new leader you're empowering? How do you know when people have risen to this level of commitment? You no longer wonder what they're doing or worry about whether they're going to deliver. You sleep well at night because you know that the leader who owns the job is the one who will lose sleep over it. That takes time, but you must give them ownership for them to get there.

6. EMPOWERING ENVIRONMENTS REWARD PRODUCTION

Do you know what always gets done? Whatever gets rewarded. In today's culture, where everyone gets a trophy for trying, that concept can sometimes get lost. Leaders who create an empowering environment reward the producers. It's always good and right to value everyone. It's always good to praise effort. But the rewards need to be given to those who produce. As Britain's former prime minister Winston Churchill said, "It's not enough that we do our best; sometimes we have to do what's required."[8] When rewards are given to productive people, they feel empowered.

HOW I EMPOWER MY LEADERS USING 10–80–10

> Leadership is like swimming. It can't be learned by reading about it. Leaders become leaders by practicing.

One of the best methods of empowerment that I've developed is something I call 10–80–10. It's a way to set leaders up for success, empower them to perform at a high level, and ensure that they cross the finish line with a victory. This is really valuable because leadership is like swimming. It can't be learned by reading about it. Leaders become leaders by practicing. An empowering leader lets them practice. I recommend you try this 10-80-10 method of empowerment as you release your new leaders to lead. Here's how it works:

THE FIRST 10 PERCENT

You've probably heard the phrase "all's well that ends well." It's the title of a play by William Shakespeare. Like many sayings coined by the playwright more than four hundred years ago, there's truth in it. But I also believe all's well that begins well. As a leader who has experience, I help the leaders who work with me to begin well so they have the best chance of ending well. How do I accomplish that? I start them off by doing five things:

1. Communicate the Objective

At the beginning of a project, I communicate the essentials so that leaders know what they need to do to get the job done:

- *The vision*—the head of the project. This tells what must be done.
- *The mission*—the heart of the project. This tells why it must be done.
- *The values*—the soul of the project. This tells the spirit in which it must be done.

The one thing I do not communicate is *how* the job must be done. That's up to those who are actually leading it. I believe in the advice of General George S. Patton, who said, "Never tell people *how* to do things. Tell them *what* to do and they will surprise you with their ingenuity."[9] I want my expectations to be clear, but I want my leaders to use creativity to fulfill them.

> "Never tell people *how* to do things. Tell them *what* to do and they will surprise you with their ingenuity."
>
> —GEORGE S. PATTON

2. Ask Questions to Help Them Plan

Few things are better at getting leaders to think than questions. I've written an entire book on the subject, called *Good Leaders Ask Great Questions*, so I won't say too much about it here. But at the very minimum, I want to emphasize these questions that I like to ask as a leader begins on a project:

- "What is the potential?" This question makes them aware of the upside, and their answers give me insight into the benefits *the leader* believes success could bring.
- "What are the potential problems?" This question reminds them of the downside, and their answers give me insight into the leader's experience, perception, and thinking process.
- "Do you have any questions?" I want to offer leaders as much information and advice as they need.
- "How can I help you?" I want leaders to know they have my support. In addition, their answer to this question gives me a sense of how much they want to rely on me, and how much independence they desire.

The specific task may require additional questions, but you get the idea. The objective is to set your leaders up for a win.

3. Provide Resources

You can't expect people to be successful if they don't have what they need to accomplish their mission. As their leader, I make sure to give them what I know they will need. Will they need more staff? Will they require additional funding? Will I need to try to connect them with another leader? I need to bring my experience to bear and help them.

4. Offer Encouragement

I believe in people, and it's my goal as a leader to help them believe in themselves. I offer encouragement and state my belief in my leaders to help them move from asking themselves, "Can I?" to asking, "How can I?" I do that by reminding them of their strengths and of what they have already accomplished. This communicates my belief in them and gives them the confidence that they can succeed.

5. Release Them to Take Ownership

As soon as I believe I've set leaders up for success, I release them to complete the objective. And I encourage them to take ownership of it. I like the way author Jim Collins looks at this. In *How the Mighty Fall*, he wrote:

> One notable distinction between wrong people and right people is that the former sees themselves as having "jobs," while the latter see themselves as having *responsibilities*. Every person in a key seat should be able to respond to the question "What do you do?" *not* with a job title, but with a statement of personal responsibility. "I'm the one person ultimately responsible for x and y."[10]

I want my leaders to think of themselves as the people who take ultimate responsibility.

There are certainly a lot of different ways to release people to take on a challenge. The Center for Organizational Effectiveness created a progressive process for releasing people. I see it as a progression of growth from new leaders to experienced ones. Look at the six levels of empowerment they outline.

Level 1: Look into it. Report. I'll decide what to do. (Least empowering.)

Level 2: Look into it. Report alternatives with pros and cons and your recommendation.

Level 3: Look into it. Let me know what you intend to do, but don't do it unless I say yes.

Level 4: Look into it. Let me know what you intend to do and do it unless I say no.

Level 5: Take action. Let me know what you did.

Level 6: Take action. No further contact required. (Most empowered.)

This is a bit mechanical, but it gives an idea of the degrees of independence different leaders might be capable of. Ideally, you want to equip leaders who are capable of starting on level 4 and coach them all the way up to level 5 or 6.

THE MIDDLE 80 PERCENT—WHERE LEADERS RISE UP TO THEIR POTENTIAL

Leadership expert Warren Bennis said, "Leadership is the capacity to translate vision into reality."[11] That's what empowered leaders do. Once they've been set up for success and released, they do what's needed to translate the vision into reality. How do they do that? Here's what I've found:

1. Empowered Leaders Add More and Better Ideas

Poet James Russell Lowell said, "[Creativity] is not in the finding of a thing, but the making something out of it after it is found."[12] The best leaders take an idea and add to it. And they encourage the members of their team to add to it. When you empower and release your leaders to be creative and innovate, they produce better results.

2. Empowered Leaders Seize Opportunities

There's an old saying: "No business opportunity is ever lost. If you fumble it, your competitor will find it." It's your job to provide your leaders with opportunities to shine. It's their job to seize those opportunities and deliver. That's how they advance the vision of the organization and how they prove themselves as leaders. You don't want them wasting their energy in fighting to *get* opportunities. You want them fighting to make the most of the opportunities you've given them.

3. Empowered Leaders Use Their Influence

Good leaders use influence, not power, to get things done. They cast vision. They build relationships. They serve others. They help their people produce. They challenge them when needed. They persuade instead of pressure. And if they ask you to lend your voice and influence to help them with this process, do it. Endorse their efforts, but allow them to be the ones making things happen.

4. Empowered Leaders Facilitate the Success of Their Teams

Good leaders don't do all of the heavy lifting themselves. That's not leading. Instead they spend a lot of time facilitating. They facilitate meetings; they facilitate the resolution of disagreements; they facilitate problem-solving. Why? Because they know that if they facilitate their people's interactions instead of giving people orders or trying to do it themselves, they will harness the team's best ideas, inspire the most participation, and receive everyone's best efforts.

Author, speaker, and communication coach Steve Adubato has said:

Great facilitation, regardless of the venue, is about creating an open, relaxed and interactive environment in which all participants feel comfortable asking questions and expressing their views.

The ability to facilitate is not something people are born with. Rather, it is something that people have to learn through coaching and practice. It is something that corporations and other organizations must be committed to if they want their meetings, seminars, workshops or employee conferences to be successful.[13]

Help your leaders develop the craft of facilitation. What do I mean by facilitating?

- Facilitating is two-way communication.
- Facilitating is interactive.
- Facilitating is exploratory.
- Facilitating is a mode to transfer information and ideas.
- Facilitating is an art form of asking open-ended questions.

When done well, facilitating brings the best out of everyone on the team. Because it is interactive, it challenges leaders to lead based upon where the people are at that moment. This enhances their leadership.

THE LAST 10 PERCENT—ALL'S WELL THAT ENDS WELL

As empowered leaders get ready to take their team across the finish line and complete the project they've been working on, this is where to get involved again. Because I want them to win, I try to do three things:

1. Add Value If Possible

One of the questions I ask myself at this phase: "Is there anything else I can add to this effort that will take us to a higher level or that will make sure we go the distance?" If there is, I do it. If I can add value by putting a final touch on the team's efforts, I want to do it. I like to think of this as adding the cherry on the top. I don't do this to take away from all the work they've done. I do it to enhance their efforts for the sake of our clients or customers.

2. Give Recognition to Them and Their Team

Psychologist William James said, "The deepest principle of human nature is the craving to be appreciated."[14] I make it a point to praise my leaders and their teams. They deserve the credit, and I want to give it to them. And the timing is important. I try to do it as soon as possible. Often this occurs in private because I want to recognize them while the "sweat is still on their brows." However, to maximize recognition, it's best to do it publicly, especially for newer leaders.

> "The deepest principle of human nature is the craving to be appreciated."
>
> —WILLIAM JAMES

3. Ask Questions to Help Them Learn from the Experience

One of the most valuable services we can do for our leaders after empowering them is to ask them questions on the back end of the process to help them gain perspective and learn from their successes and failures. Here are the three questions I ask more often:

"How was your experience?" Too many leaders finish a task and never assess the process they went through. They simply dash off to accomplish the next thing. Don't let them. Prompt them to stop, think, and assess. If things went poorly, but they say everything went well, I discover that there's a disconnect, and I need to help them become more self-aware. If things went well, but all they see are the negatives, I learn that I need to coach them up. The most rewarding conversations reveal both the good and the bad.

"What did you learn?" I want every empowered experience of my leaders to be a learning experience. This question prompts leaders to reach for the lesson in both success and failure. As I've always said: experience isn't the best teacher—evaluated experience is.

"What would you do differently next time?" This final question gets leaders thinking proactively. They begin to anticipate how they will apply what they've learned. That's an important growth step. It helps them shift from thinking, "I'm glad that's over," to "I can't wait until I get to try this again."

The 10–80–10 method doesn't work in every situation or with every leader. But it's been highly effective for me. I recommend you try it with your new leaders and see how it works. If you can set people on a good course, release them to achieve in their own way, and then help them learn on the back end, it's a win for everyone.

There is an art to empowering leaders, and if your personality is not an especially outgoing, positive, or encouraging, you will have to work hard to create an empowering environment where you release people to succeed, praise them, and give them credit. But you can do it. And that's essential, because leaders will not develop to their potential if you don't let them lead.

ACTION STEPS

1. How secure are you as a leader? How do you respond when your colleagues or your team members receive praise and credit? Do you celebrate with and for them? Or are you secretly—or not so secretly—resentful? If you harbor feelings of resentment, you must work through and resolve those feelings to become an empowering leader. Examine why other people's success threatens you. Talk to other leaders who are positive when others succeed to learn how they think. Seek counseling if needed. Learn how to support and empower your team members and leaders.

2. Create an empowering environment for the members of your team. For each of the characteristics of such an environment, identify what actions you will take to promote them. Be as specific as possible in your planning.

   - **Embrace Everyone's Potential**
   - **Give Team Members Freedom**
   - **Encourage Collaboration**
   - **Promote Accountability**
   - **Give Your Leadership Ownership**
   - **Reward Production**

3. Try using to 10-80-10 of leadership empowerment with your new leaders. For each project a new leader attempts, do the following:

The First 10 Percent
- Communicate the Objective
- Ask Questions to Help Them Plan
- Provide Resources
- Offer Encouragement
- Release them to Take Ownership

The Middle 80 Percent
- Observe Their Efforts
- Encourage Them
- Coach Them if Needed

The Last 10 Percent
- Add Value if Possible
- Give Recognition to Them and Their Team
- Ask Questions to Help Them Learn from the Experience

---

4. Spend time reflecting on the experience by evaluate the leader's performance and the effectiveness of the 10-80-10 method.

- How can you help that leader to further develop?
- What can you do to help that leader be more successful next time?
- How can you change your method of empowerment to improve it?

NINE

HARNESS YOUR LEADERS' NATURAL MOTIVATION

One of the questions leaders ask me most is, "How can I motivate my people?" There's a good reason for that. In every leader's organization or team you can find people who seem to lack motivation. It can be difficult to get some people moving. Ideally, the leaders you have chosen and begun developing will not be reluctant to dive into challenges and take action. But even people with high potential can use a boost. All of us can benefit from a bit of motivation from time to time.

IS MOTIVATION INTERNAL OR EXTERNAL?

Daniel Pink has written an excellent book on motivation, called *Drive*. He opens the book by recounting an experiment with rhesus monkeys conducted in 1949 by psychology professor Harry F. Harlow and two colleagues at the University of Wisconsin. They wanted to gain insight into how primates learned, so they conducted an experiment in which the monkeys were given a puzzle to solve. But the three behavioral scientists learned something unexpected about motivation.

At that time, the scientific community attributed motivation to either biological needs or external incentives. They believed internal biological motivation came down to the desire for food, water, or sex. The external motivations came from rewards and punishments. But what they discovered was that the monkeys in their experiment solved the puzzle they were given simply for the enjoyment of completing the process.

Pink said Harlow's conclusion, which was a radical notion at the time, was that primates, including humans, possessed a third driving factor in motivation. Performing a task could provide its own intrinsic reward: "The monkeys solved the puzzles simply because they found it gratifying to solve puzzles."[1]

I think anyone who has ever enjoyed doing a task for its own sake—playing golf, learning to play a song, building a ship in a bottle—would think this makes sense. Yet Pink said the findings "should have changed the world—but did not."[2] What may be more surprising is what another researcher, Edward Deci, discovered when he did follow-up experiments gauging motivation twenty years later. In these experiments, Deci asked university students to solve puzzles. Some of them he incentivized with monetary rewards, and others he didn't. Pink wrote:

> Human motivation seemed to operate by laws that ran counter to what most scientists and citizens believed. From the office to the playing field, we knew what got people going. Rewards—especially cold, hard cash—intensified interest and enhanced performance. What Deci

found, and then confirmed in two additional studies he conducted shortly thereafter, was almost the opposite. "When money is used as an external reward for some activity, the subjects lose intrinsic interest for the activity," he wrote. Rewards can deliver a short-term boost—just as a jolt of caffeine can keep you cranking for a few more hours. But the effect wears off—and, worse, can reduce a person's longer-term motivation to continue the project. . . . [Deci concluded,] "One who is interested in developing and enhancing intrinsic motivation in children, employees, students, etc., should not concentrate on external-control systems."[3]

Now, back to the question I mentioned at the beginning of this chapter. When people ask me how I motivate my people, my answer is that I don't. I don't try to push or pull people. Instead, I try to inspire people and help them harness their own motivations. After they've discovered their own internal motivations, I encourage them to fan that spark into a roaring fire. Finally, I try to coach them to a place where tapping into their own internal motivations is a habit. If you've done the work of getting to know your leaders as individuals and learned more about them at the leadership table, you should already have a sense of what matters to them and how they are motivated. If they don't already recognize what that is, your task as their developer is to help them discover it and tap into it.

THE SEVEN MOTIVATIONS OF LEADERS

Daniel Pink identifies three internal motivations that move people forward. But after decades of working with people, I made my own list of seven motivations. Three are the same as Pink's. As you work with your leaders, I believe you will observe one or more of these "sparks" within each person you work with. Your job is to find the sparks and fuel them. When you do that, people will not only work hard—they will also work smart, because their work and their motivation are aligned.

1. Purpose—Leaders Want to Do What They Were Created to Do

By far the strongest motivator I've seen in people is purpose. The human spirit comes alive when it finds a cause worth fighting for. With purpose, people's *have-to* life turns into a *want-to* life. They live for a cause, not for applause.

Unfortunately, many people have not discovered their purpose, and as a result, they aren't living for something larger than themselves. When people believe nothing is truly good, right, and worth striving and sacrificing for, their lives can feel meaningless, barren. They lack persistence and a positive sense of self. And no matter what actions they take or work they do, they don't feel better about themselves or increase their self-worth. But when they feel a sense of purpose, everything changes.

About ten years ago, I read a column by Peggy Noonan in which she recounted a conversation between Clare Boothe Luce and John F. Kennedy. It occurred in the White House in 1962. According to Noonan:

> [Luce] told him . . . that "a great man is one sentence." His leadership can be so well summed up in a single sentence that you don't have to hear his name to know who's being talked about. "He preserved the union and freed the slaves," or, "He lifted us out of a great depression and helped to win a World War." You didn't have to be told "Lincoln" or "FDR."
>
> She wondered what Kennedy's sentence would be. She was telling him to concentrate, to know the great themes and demands of his time and focus on them.[4]

When I read something like that, it's catalytic for me. It makes me immediately ask myself, "What is my one sentence?" Does it do the same to you? When I search myself for an answer, my one sentence is: I add value to leaders who multiply value to others. For that reasons, I work to be a catalyst for transformation, to help develop leaders to change the world around them.

What's your sentence? If you already know it and are living it, you'll be in a better place to help your leaders find their purpose. Here are some questions to help you and them start the discovery process.

- **Talent:** What do you do well?
- **Desire:** What do you want to do?
- **Recognition:** What do others say you do well?
- **Results:** What do you do that has a productive return?
- **Growth:** What do you do that you can keep getting better at doing?

When a leader answers those questions—and the answers need only be a sentence, phrase, or couple of words—and the answers begin to align, they point to purpose. Here's what I mean. If leaders' talents and what they want to do aren't compatible, they have not yet discovered their purpose. If what they put as their talent isn't what others say they do well, then their view of their talent may not be accurate. If they can't get better at what they want to do, it's probably not their purpose. When talent, desire, recognition, and growth all line up, and those factors are affirmed and recognized by others, they are probably doing what they were created to do. Otherwise, they need to keep searching.

Your responsibility as a developer of leaders is to walk people through this process of asking questions and help them answer honestly. Many executives, even those at the highest levels of organizations, don't see themselves clearly. They don't know their own strengths and weaknesses. As a result, they don't find their purpose.

When you know why you've been put on this earth and you know what you need to be doing, you don't need anyone to motivate you. Your purpose inspires you every day. Furthermore, you can make a difference. George Washington Carver asserted, "No individual has any right to come into the world and go out of it without leaving behind him distinct and legitimate reasons for having passed through it."[5] Knowing their purpose helps leaders make a positive impact on their world.

2. AUTONOMY—LEADERS WANT THE FREEDOM TO CONTROL THEIR LIVES

Over the years I've had the privilege of speaking to people in many direct-sales organizations all around the world. I always enjoy it because their enthusiasm is off the charts. Depending on the group and location, their products may be different and the cultures of the countries where they live and work may be unique, but they have one thing in common. They love having freedom—freedom to choose their business path, freedom to make their own decisions about how they work, and freedom to determine their personal potential. And I can tell you, when I visit a country where people had few freedoms in the past and they get a chance to experience a degree of autonomy, they seize the opportunity. And they are much happier and more productive as a result.

If you look back into the history of the United States, you can see the power of freedom. For example, historian Joseph P. Cullen wrote:

When the English founded the settlement at Jamestown in 1607, the colony operated under a communal system. Everything was held in a kind of common ownership, and about half of the community for the first few years was made up of gentlemen who generally chose not to work.

When John Smith became President of the group, he noted what II Thessalonians 3:10 said and made a rule "that he that will not work, shall not eat, except by sickness he be disabled." Productivity suddenly shot up. Later, Sir Thomas Dale took command of the group and ruled that deserving individuals could have a few acres for private planting, and a diary from the time indicates that "wee reaped not so much come from the labours of thirtie as now three or foure doe provide for themselves."[6]

Do you see the pattern there? When people had the freedom to make choices and were rewarded for their efforts, productivity went up nearly tenfold.

Daniel Pink explored the power of having autonomy in *Drive*. He cited a Cornell University study of 320 small businesses in which half of the businesses gave people autonomy to do their work and the other half used top-down direction with their employees. You can probably guess which group did better. But would you be surprised to find out that the businesses that offered autonomy grew at four times the rate of the other businesses and had only one-third of the turnover?[7]

I like having options in life, and I believe most other leaders do too. When your leaders have demonstrated that they can work independently, then give them more autonomy and watch to see how they respond.

3. Relationships—Leaders Want to Do Things with Other People

One of my great pleasures in life is getting to do something that matters with people who matter to me. In my book *Winning with People*, I wrote about the Partnership Principle, which says that working together increases the odds of winning together.[8] But I would add to that, working together increases the joy of working.

I cannot imagine doing life without others. Teamwork truly does make the dream work. Relationships inspire me, and I believe this is true for most good leaders. Furthermore, I believe personal transformation comes when we give ourselves to a cause greater than ourselves and believe in its possibilities to make a difference. That transformation goes to a whole new level when we find our people, lock arms with them, and work together to reach for a positive impact that is just beyond our grasp.

> The Partnership Principle: working together increases the odds of winning together.

Give your leaders opportunities to work with people they like. Prompt them to make connections with members of their teams. Encourage them to find joy in the journey with others as they work to achieve their goals.

4. PROGRESS—LEADERS WANT TO EXPERIENCE PERSONAL AND PROFESSIONAL GROWTH

When I was a young leader just starting off in my career, a mentor told me, "Spend your life being *for* something and running *to* something." I think he said that because he saw that I was always working hard, but too often I was spinning my wheels. And if you think about it, you only make progress if you're getting traction, not just because your wheels are turning.

What is *traction* but *track* plus *action*? A track is a planned path that we want to run on. Action is what we do that gets results. The old saying is true: even if we are on the right track, we will get run over if we just sit there. Having a clear track and taking action give us traction so we can go where we want to go.

My mentor's words resonated with me. I've always enjoyed achievement. And when I realized that progress came from growth, it changed my life, especially when I paired my desire for growth with consistency. I wanted to improve, so I got intentional about learning and never quit. I didn't have any sudden big hits early in my career. I wasn't a "home run hitter." My secret was getting up to bat every day and trying to get on base.

I've discussed growth a lot in this book because it's what most people need to turn their dreams into reality. Your leaders need to grow in small, regular, incremental steps. You need to help them take them. They can follow the advice of John Wooden, who used to tell his players to make each day their masterpiece.[9] If they grow every day, day after day, their lives can become masterpieces.

5. MASTERY—LEADERS WANT TO EXCEL AT THEIR WORK

The desire for personal and professional growth often leads to the next source of motivation that inspires many leaders: the desire for mastery. No one can achieve mastery who is not continually growing. Ongoing growth doesn't guarantee mastery, but if you're not growing and working at getting better, you have no shot at experiencing the exhilaration that comes from being great at what you do. As NBA coach and general manager Pat Riley said, "Excellence is the gradual result of always striving to do better."[10]

> "Excellence is the gradual result of always striving to do better."
>
> —PAT RILEY

When I started my career in my first formal leadership role, I realized that if I wanted to, I could get by without having to put in too much effort. People naturally liked me, I was a good talker, and I had a lot of energy, especially when it came to public speaking. I was very tempted to wing it instead of working at it. Just a few months into the job, I made a decision. I would not take shortcuts. I would not cut corners. Even in situations where people advised me that

I could take an easier route, I wouldn't. I would tap into my passion for excellence and continually work to get better at my craft.

Tapping into the desire for mastery as a motivation—and encouraging your leaders to find their own inspiration in mastery—requires the right mind-set. It's an attitude. In his classic comic strip *Calvin and Hobbes*, cartoonist Bill Watterson put the following words in the mouth of six-year-old Calvin:

> We don't value craftsmanship anymore! All we value is ruthless efficiency, and I say we deny our own humanity that way! Without appreciation for grace and beauty, there's no pleasure in having them! Our lives are made drearier, rather than richer! How can a person take pride in his work when skill and care are considered luxuries! We're not machines! We have a human need for craftsmanship![11]

Now truthfully, in this case, Calvin was making excuses to his teacher for not turning in a paper, but what he says still communicates the idea that striving for mastery is like developing craftsmanship. It takes time and attention. Every opportunity to work is an opportunity to perfect your craft. That doesn't mean you will ever achieve perfection. Neither will the people you lead. But you can still be intentional and strive for it.

A couple of years ago, I went to dinner at The French Laundry restaurant in Napa Valley, California. Eating there was an unforgettable experience. It's not surprising that the restaurant is considered one of the best in the world. Everything is done with excellence. The setting is beautiful, the staff is extraordinary, the service is superb, and the food is spectacular. After our dinner, we had the privilege of taking a private tour of the wine cellar and the kitchen. As the chefs and cooks worked calmly and quietly, we recognized that we were watching the best of the best. As we were about to leave, I noticed that a large clock hung on the wall, visible for all the staff. Beneath the clock were the words, "Sense of Urgency." It was a constant reminder of intentionality for them.

Mastery is never fully realized by anyone. We all fall short. But striving for mastery allows us to continually push forward and improve. Leaders who tap into this aspect of motivation know they'll never cross the finish line of perfection, but they're getting better all the time, and they find the pursuit of excellence fulfilling.

6. RECOGNITION—LEADERS WANT OTHERS TO APPRECIATE THEIR ACCOMPLISHMENTS

Many years ago, psychologist Henry H. Goddard conducted a study on energy levels in children, using an instrument he called the "ergo-graph." He discovered that when tired children were commended or praised, the ergograph measured an instant energy surge in the children. When they were harshly spoken to or criticized, the ergograph measured an immediate, significant decrease in their physical energy.

Goddard's research reveals a truth, not just about children but about every human being, including leaders. Everyone desires to be recognized, praised, and appreciated. As you lead and motivate others, never forget that. Recognize and praise their work. Let them know you appreciate their accomplishments.

7. MONEY—LEADERS WANT TO BE FINANCIALLY SECURE

The last motivator I want to talk about is money. Radio comedian Fred Allen said, "There are many things more important than money. And they all cost money."[12] That's a funny line. But while money is first on many people's list, it's not on mine. For me it happens to be the lowest of all motivators.

I do think wanting financial security is a worthy goal. The best thing money can buy is financial freedom, which gives a person options. But money is a powerful motivator only until you have enough to get what you want. It may have great pull up until then, but after you achieve certain financial goals, its appeal lessens—that is, unless you have a better plan for it.

Once you've achieved your financial goals, my suggestion is to begin focusing on giving. When you experience the joy of giving and develop the mind-set that you can be a river instead of a reservoir with your wealth and help others, then earning money can continue to be a powerful motivator. Many successful leaders I know think of their finances in this way.

WHICH MOTIVATORS CONNECT?

As you develop leaders, learn which of these seven factors motivate them and tap into them. A mistake I made as a young leader was thinking that I should try to lead everyone the way I wanted to be led. I took what motivated me and tried to motivate others with it. That was a mistake because they weren't me! You can't be a good leader and lead everyone the same. It's actually a demotivator.

By learning what motivates your leaders and harnessing that motivation, you will energize them to keep growing and developing. Focus first on what motivates them the most, but also inspire them in every area you can. Help them discover their purpose. Give them as much autonomy as you can. Build strong relationships with them and help them to foster good relationships with others. Provide them with opportunities and resources to grow. Encourage and incentivize them to strive toward mastery of their skills. Praise them. And reward them financially.

FROM MOTIVATION TO HABIT

As a leader, you want to inspire people to tap into their own internal motivation, but researchers say that this has its limits. Why? Because it's often driven by emotion, and that's not sustainable over the long haul. Stephen Guise, author of *Mini Habits*, said:

> When you're first starting a new goal, you'll be excited and highly motivated to start strong. But the more consistent your progress, the lower your general motivation is likely to be over time. **This is because of habits. . . .**
>
> The secret of super athletes isn't that they're "super motivated." . . . The thing that really sets the elite apart is how they're able to train when they're bored out of their minds or tired. Their routines and schedules keep them in top shape. . . .
>
> Super athletes don't let their training schedule depend on their current motivation level, and that's why they succeed.[13]

I like to think of motivation as giving the power to sprint. The problem is that to be successful at anything, including leading, we need to be marathoners. That ability comes only with the development of habits that will keep us going and improving.

So, go ahead and start by connecting your people to as many of the seven motivators as you can. That will help them start moving forward and developing momentum. But also set them up for success by teaching positive work habits. For years I have used the acronym BEST to do this:

Believe in them.

Encourage them.

Show them.

Train them.

The idea is to train them to do what's right and to help them do it consistently until it becomes a habit. People don't determine their future; they determine their habits, which determine their future. If you can help your leaders to obtain habits of success, they'll do right then feel right, instead of waiting to feel right before doing right. The habits they form by doing the right things without feeling motivation on the front end will fuel them to keep going on the back end. The more they do the right things, the greater the skill they'll develop, and the more they will enjoy what they do. As writer John Ruskin said, "When love and skill work together, expect a masterpiece."[14]

> People don't determine their future. They determine their habits, which determine their future.

The best leaders and highest achievers are always self-motivated. They work because they want to. They lead others because it's rewarding. They take joy in their work. One of the greatest gifts you can give as a developer of leaders is to help the people you lead to harness their own internal motivation so that they can lead and inspire others every day. Self-motivation helps leaders take the focus off themselves and put it on the people they lead.

ACTION STEPS

1. You will be better able to understand the motivations of your leaders if you understand your own. Review the seven motivators in this chapter. Rank them in order of importance to you from first to last:

   - Purpose—I want to do what I was created to do
   - Autonomy—I want the freedom to control my life
   - Relationships—I want to do things with other people
   - Progress—I want to experience personal and professional growth
   - Mastery—I want to excel at my work
   - Recognition—I want others to appreciate my accomplishments
   - Money—I want to be financially secure

   What do your answers teach you about yourself?

   _____

2. Think about each of your leaders. What do you think motivates them based on what you've observed? Try to identify what you believe to be each person's primary motivation.

   _____

3. Talk with your leaders. Present the seven motivators. Ask them whether they believe there are other important motivators not in this list. Then ask them to rank their personal motivations from first to last. Write the rankings for each leader here:

   _____

Leader	Purpose	Autonomy	Relationships	Progress	Mastery	Recognition	Money

4. Develop a strategy to help each leader tap into their motivators, starting with their primary one. Do whatever you can to facilitate their access to that motivation. And help them to develop habits that will keep them engaged and motivated during the times they experience a lull in energy or inspiration.

TEN

CHALLENGE YOUR LEADERS
TO WORK AS A TEAM

What's more powerful than a motivated, equipped, and empowered leader? A group of motivated, equipped, and empowered leaders. What's more powerful than that? That same group of motivated, equipped, and empowered leaders *working as a team*! When good leaders are gathered together, empowered by a leader, focused on a vision, and working *together* as a team, there's almost nothing they can't do.

If you have committed to being a developer of people and are developing leaders consistently, whether you do it one leader at a time or you work with several potential leaders and develop them together, you will eventually develop a *group* of leaders. To take them to the next level in their development, you'll want to develop them into a *team* of leaders. But I have to warn you; that can be a challenge. Why? Leaders are hard to gather. And it can be a challenge to get them to work together. They all have their own ideas, and they would usually rather be the leader of

> "A dream is a compelling vision you see in your heart that is too big to accomplish without the help of others."
>
> —CHRIS HODGES

the team than a member of one. But it will be worth it, because a good team is greater than the sum of its parts.

A good team of *leaders* has the potential to accomplish great dreams. I love what my friend Chris Hodges says about dreams. He says a dream is "a compelling vision you see in your heart that is too big to accomplish without the help of others." That's why anyone with a dream needs a team.

If you have a dream and no team—the dream is impossible.
If you have a dream and a bad team—the dream is a nightmare.
If you have a dream and are building a team—the dream is possible.
If you have a dream and a good leadership team—the dream is inevitable.

HOW TO CREATE A TEAM OF LEADERS

If you want to achieve big things and develop your leaders at the same time, then you need to challenge them to work together as a team. To do that, do these five things:

1. MAKE SURE YOUR LEADERS ARE IN ALIGNMENT WITH THE VISION

Marcus Buckingham has studied teams for decades, focusing on what makes them excellent. Over the years, he has found what he calls eight factors of high-performing teams. He has arranged them in a chart showing how successful people respond in each area related to the team's and their own personal needs.

Area	"We" Needs	"Me" Needs
	I am really enthusiastic about the mission of my company.	At work, I clearly understand what is expected of me.
	In my team, I am surrounded by people who share my values.	I have a chance to use my strengths every day at work.
	My teammates have my back.	I know I will be recognized for excellent work.
	I have great confidence in my company's future.	In my work, I am always challenged to grow.[1]

I believe Buckingham's observations are really about alignment. On great teams, players' individual purposes, goals, and values align with those of the organization and the other players. If you look at each area on Buckingham's chart, you can see members of an excellent team embrace the organization's purpose and understand how their own purpose aligns with it. They believe their values and strengths align with those of the team. They feel supported by the organization and their fellow team members. And they see a positive future ahead for both themselves and the organization. Everyone is on the same page and going the same direction.

This kind of alignment doesn't happen by accident. It has to be facilitated by the leader of the team. You must communicate to help your leaders make the connections between the vision, the team, and their own strengths and desires. Clarify each leader's contribution. Help every leader appreciate the other leaders' contributions. Coach and mentor them. Find ways to communicate creatively and continually.

2. HELP YOUR LEADERS BOND AND CARE FOR ONE ANOTHER

Examine any successful team, and you will find people who care about each other and possess relational and emotional bondedness. This is evident in combat units in the military, and especially on special forces teams, such as the Navy SEALs or British Commandos. Members of the team fight for one another under the most extreme circumstances and are even willing to die for one another. But bondedness is also evident in less extreme environments, such as on championship teams in sports and high-achieving teams in business and volunteer organizations.

Consultant Paul Arnold shared insights that researchers have discovered about the impact of team bondedness. Arnold wrote:

Shah and Jehn (1993) from Kellogg's Graduate School and Wharton studied a group of people from the first year of an MBA class. They asked everyone to write down who they most got on well with, and then divided half the group into teams of people who got on well together and the other half were then randomly assigned. In a series of tests, unsurprisingly the team made up of those who got on well together outperformed the other team. The surprise was by the sheer extent—in a very mundane task, they outperformed the other team by 20% and the more complex task by 70%. When they investigated further they found two key factors: The first was that in the team that bonded, there was **more support** for each other—especially important in the mundaneness of the first task—spirits were kept high. In the second, more complex task the other key factor came out—there were arguments. In the un-bonded team, no one really wanted to upset anyone else, so the discussions were cordial, resulting in *compromised decision* making. In the team that bonded, the friendship allowed for real arguments on the content to take place, without it spilling over into personal attacks. Thus, out of this healthy debate, **better decisions** were made.

So, in conclusion, any group who wants to perform at a high level, needs to more closely bond (at an emotional level).[2]

So how can you facilitate emotional connection and bondedness among leaders on your team? It starts with trust. That is the foundation for connection, growth, and teamwork. Mike Krzyzewski, head coach of the Duke University men's basketball team, advised, "If you set up an atmosphere of communication and trust, it becomes a tradition. Older team members will establish your credibility with newer ones. Even if they don't like everything about you, they'll still say, 'He's trustworthy, committed to us as a team.'"[3] When you can lay that groundwork, you can foster trust and start building connections.

Pat Lencioni has written extensively on teams. I love what he said about trust in his book *The Five Dysfunctions of a Team*. Members of trusting teams

- Admit weaknesses and mistakes
- Ask for help
- Accept questions and input about their areas of responsibility
- Give one another the benefit of the doubt before arriving at a negative conclusion
- Take risks in offering feedback and assistance
- Appreciate and tap into one another's skills and experiences
- Focus time and energy on important issues, not politics
- Offer and accept apologies without hesitation
- Look forward to meetings and other opportunities to work as a group[4]

The bottom line in caring for others on the team is that it's crucial to give more than you take. If you care about teammates and you have an emotional connection, a bond, with one another, you focus on being generous. You find ways to add value to the team and your teammates. You're not just in it for yourself, only after what you can get—even at the expense of other team members.

Gayle D. Beebe wrote an insightful book on the shaping of effective leaders. Basing his ideas on insights gleaned from Peter Drucker, the father of modern management, he used the terms *greed* and *generosity* when discussing the behavior of people in an organization and their impact on team atmosphere and results. Beebe wrote:

> Greed destroys community. Greed essentially has no limit. Greed is boundless in its grasping for money or fame. Eventually it leads to a lack of respect for the needs and ambitions of others because our own needs and ambitions overrun all normal boundaries and expectations. It is particularly corrosive on teams, and when present in senior executives, greed can destroy whole organizations. It is made manifest by an excessive need for acclaim, attention, or compensation. It also is evident in an inability to share the limelight. Malice and thoughtlessness are twin manifestations of this same inner drive. Its root is a boundless craving that exceeds all capacity for satisfaction.
>
> Generosity, on the other hand, builds community. Generosity allows us to give and receive because we are free from domination by money or fame. . . . Generosity also gives us the ability to handle . . . the ups and downs that come to each one of us—in ways that have a positive and enduring outcome.[5]

Teams of leaders who trust one another, who are connected to one another, and who are bonded enough give more than they take can to communicate with each other and be highly productive. The road may not always be smooth. Team members may not always agree with each other. But they work together, and they talk it out when they have problems. That's important because, as my friend Mark Sanborn said, "In teamwork, silence isn't golden, it's deadly."[6]

As the leader of a leadership team, you are responsible for helping everyone connect, get to know one another, and work together. As teammates become sure of themselves and sure of other team members both professionally and personally, the group will start to become more of a team. Bonded teams become building teams.

> "In teamwork,
> silence isn't golden,
> it's deadly."
>
> —MARK SANBORN

3. Ensure That Your Leaders Are Growing Together

One of the best ways to bond team members and give them a brighter future is to make sure they experience growth together. Several years ago, I created an acronym to help me design growth plans for members of my leadership team:

Give them a growth environment.
Recognize each person's growth needs.
Open up opportunities for them to grow.
Walk with them in challenging times.
Teach them to learn from every experience.
Help them add value to their teammates.

Let's look at each of the six parts of this process in turn.

Give Your Leaders a Growth Environment

When I first realized the importance of growth, not only for myself but also for the members of my team, I sat down and crafted a description of what kind of situation promoted growth. Here's my description of a growth environment that benefits a team. It is a place where . . .

- Others are ahead of them
- They are continually challenged
- Their focus is forward
- The atmosphere is affirming
- They are out of your comfort zone
- They wake up excited
- Failure is not their enemy
- Others are growing
- People desire change
- Growth is expected

If you want the leaders on your team to grow, you need to work to create an environment like the one I describe. That begins with you, because as the leader, you can facilitate many of the things listed. You can model growth and stay ahead of your leaders. You can expect growth, promote change, and challenge people. You can ask them to get out of their comfort zone and allow them to fail safely. And you can encourage them. Do all these things, and they will be more likely to do their part.

Recognize Each Leader's Growth Needs

As you have gotten to know, equipped, and developed your leaders, you've come to understand their strengths and weakness, and you've talked with them about how they need to grow. Take this process to the next stage. Every year, ask teach member to share two areas in which they desire to grow in the coming year. I do this every December with the leaders on my team. Often the areas they identify line up with or correspond to those that I observe. If they don't, we discuss them. The goal is to agree on what we will work on for the next twelve months.

Including your leaders in this process and responding positively to their growth aspirations creates high motivation in them. You can't dictate motivation. When people get to *weigh in* on their development, they more readily *buy in* to owning their personal growth progress.

> When people get to *weigh in* on their development, they more readily *buy in* to owning their personal growth progress.

Arrange Opportunities for Your Leaders to Grow

When you're working with leaders and helping them grow, one size does not fit all. All leaders are different, with their own background and their own set of experiences, influences, and perspectives. And the higher the level of leader, the more individual that leader's growth plan needs to be.

After I understand the growth needs of my leadership team members, I work with them to craft a plan that will support their development, and I take an active part in helping them. For example, if leaders need to grow in the area of networking, I will introduce them to people who will help and stretch them. If they need more experience leading, I will hand off a project that I know will prompt them to grow where they need it. If they lack vision, I will introduce them to experiences and people who will inspire them to dream and aspire for more. No matter what kind of growth they need, I focus offer them opportunities to meet people, go places, and receive experiences that will meet that growth need and help them blossom.

Walk with Your Leaders in Challenging Times

I've observed that difficult times offer the greatest growth experiences. Why? Because challenges cause us to seek help, become open to new ideas, and make changes that help us come out on the other side. When your leaders experience challenging times, you have the ability to add value to them if you're willing to walk alongside them and help them get through those challenges.

I find it especially satisfying to help young leaders because they are so open to assistance. I let them know they are not alone. I try to give them confidence when things are shaky. I offer perspective if they've lost their way. And I answer whatever questions they ask. Not only am I able to help them grow, but often our friendship deepens in a way that marks us forever. If you see a leader's difficulty as a time to compassionately help and gently redirect—not a time to admonish and correct—you will be able to help them in ways that positively impact their lives.

Teach Leaders to Learn from Every Experience

I believe every experience has something it can teach us. But too many people fail to learn from their experiences because they focus on their losses and not the lessons. When I want to help my leaders become better team members, I put the emphasis on the lessons. In chapter 9, I explained how I use 10–80–10 with individual leaders. Part of that process is asking questions on the back end. I like to do that with my *team* as well. After an experience together, whether positive or negative, I teach my team to assess it. We ask ourselves, "What went right? What went wrong? What did we learn? How can we improve?" Shared experiences are great opportunities for leaders to grow together as a team. Asking and answering questions in a group helps facilitate that.

Help Leaders Add Value to Their Teammates

There is no doubt that leaders and achievers tend to be highly competitive and like to win. Sometimes as a team leader, you must challenge individuals who are accustomed to winning on their own to win together as a team. That's especially true if they possess what could be called a zero-sum mind-set. I like the way *zero-sum* is explained by Investopedia:

> Zero-sum is a situation in game theory in which one person's gain is equivalent to another's loss, so the net change in wealth or benefit is zero. . . .
>
> Poker and gambling are popular examples of zero-sum games since the sum of the amounts won by some players equals the combined losses of the others. Games like chess and tennis, where there is one winner and one loser, are also zero-sum games. . . .
>
> Zero-sum games are the opposite of win-win situations—such as a trade agreement that significantly increases trade between two nations—or lose-lose situations, like war for instance.[7]

Good leaders teach that for one member to win, others on the team don't necessarily have to lose. Any time team members help each other grow or add value to one another in any way, this doesn't take away from them personally. It multiplies the entire team. Retired NBA coach Phil Jackson, who won two NBA championships as a player and eleven as a coach, said his team's motto one season was, "The strength of the Pack is the Wolf, and the strength of the Wolf is the Pack."[8] Everyone on the team was in it together. That's the kind of mind-set you want to instill in the members of your leadership team. They need to understand that nobody gets there until everybody gets there.

> "The strength of the Pack is the Wolf, and the strength of the Wolf is the Pack."
>
> —PHIL JACKSON

4. POSITION YOUR LEADERS TO COMPLEMENT AND COMPLETE ONE ANOTHER

I've written quite a bit about the mentoring sessions I had the privilege of experiencing with Coach John Wooden because they made such a great impression on me. In one of those meetings, I asked him how he was able to get so many great players to play so well together.

"It's not easy," he stated simply. And then he said something I'll never forget. "Each player must have a place for himself and a purpose beyond himself." What a perfect description of team players!

The Law of the Niche in *The 17 Indisputable Laws of Teamwork* states that all players have a place where they add the most value.[9] That place is where their greatest strengths can be utilized best and where they make their best contribution to the team. I like what consultant Ana Loback said about the importance of team members knowing where they fit on a team and the benefits that come from it:

Our research indicates that teams with better awareness of their strengths have a significant advantage, perform better and ultimately have a more positive environment that fosters trust amongst the team members.

Ambiguity breeds mistrust and it generates feelings of insecurity. The greater the clarity about roles and responsibilities and also about what energizes and motivates everyone in the team, the easier it is for individuals to know what to expect and what is expected of them.

Knowing your own strengths but also those of your teammates can help build awareness of what energizes and motivates the team as a whole but also how you can complement each other in areas of strength.

Sharing your strengths with each other, [letting others know] what you can be called on for, can create a more positive environment that fosters collaboration and commitment. Sharing your performance risks as well, what you can be called out for, puts everything out in the open, building trust and improving communication.[10]

As the team leader, you need to facilitate this process. Or as John Wooden would have said, "I help my players find their shooting spot and set them up for success." As the leader of a team of leaders, you need to do something similar. What does that take?

Know What the Job Requires

For you to be able to position your leaders on the team, you need to know what each position requires. What skills and abilities will be required for your leaders to get a job or project done? If you don't know from experience, then ask your team to help you analyze this, and then you facilitate the discussion.

Know Whose Strengths Fit the Job

If you know your leaders well, you know their talents, skills, strengths, and weaknesses, and you understand their personalities and temperaments, then you can make a good judgment call about who best fits each role. This is where all the work you've previously done developing your leaders really pays off. Too often, leaders who don't take the time to get to know their people just throw someone at a job and hope for the best. That's no way to lead a team.

As you position leaders on your team, keep in mind two considerations. Who can best do each job? And how well will leaders work together and complement one another if you put them in those jobs? The interaction of team members impacts the success of the team as much as the effectiveness of the people in their roles.

Know When to Make Adjustments

Team leaders earn their keep by making the right adjustments at the right time. Often, it's an intuitive thing. You need to give your leaders enough time and space to work things out and be successful. But you also need to know when it's time to make a change. If you pull leaders out of a role too soon, they can lose confidence and credibility with teammates. If you wait too long, the team suffers and you lose credibility with the other leaders on the team.

When should you make a change? If you can coach the struggling leader through completion of the task, that's the ideal solution. Then you can make changes afterward. However, sometimes you will need to make the change sooner. For example, if the job or task is changing and the leader is failing because he no longer fits the role, or if the leader is changing and no longer can do the job, you'll have to ask a different leader to do it.

5. Communicate to Your Leaders How They Are Making a Difference

Another step you need to take to help your leaders become better as a team is to help position them mentally. Many people don't really see the purpose in their work. They see themselves as employees with a job description who need to fulfill a work assignment. Lift up members of your team by making sure they how their work matters. Sometimes discouraged people just need to see how the work they do makes a difference in this world. That requires a mental shift, not a job change.

David Sturt, executive vice president of O.C. Tanner, wrote in *Forbes* about a study done of people in jobs that are considered low-level and unsung. What the researchers found was enlightening:

In 2001, Jane [Dutton] and her colleague Amy Wrzesniewski from Yale began to study how people in unglamorous jobs were coping with what they call "devalued work." When they tried to think of supposedly unrewarding jobs to study, they chose hospital janitors. But what they learned from their studies took them completely by surprise and changed the trajectory of their research for the coming decade.

As Jane and Amy interviewed the cleaning staff of a major hospital in the Midwest, they discovered that a certain subset of housekeepers didn't see themselves as part of the janitorial staff at all.

They saw themselves as part of the professional staff, as part of the healing team. And that changed everything. These people would get to know patients and families and offer support in small but important ways: A box of Kleenex here or a glass of water there. A word of encouragement. . . .

People often take existing job expectations—or job descriptions—and expand them to suit their desire to make a difference. . . . [They] do what's expected (because it's required) and then find a way to add something new to their work.[11]

These people lifted *themselves* up mentally and emotionally by deciding their work mattered. They recognized they were making a difference.

As the leader of your team, you can lift up the members of your team. Positioning your leaders means doing more than finding their passions and strengths and placing them into the right roles. You can help them position their minds to think differently about their work. You can encourage them to think more about others and less about themselves, to start their day sowing into others by intentionally adding value to their teammates every day without focusing on reaping a harvest for themselves.

How much time will it take you to get your leaders to work together as a team? That depends. How cooperative were they before they became leaders? How competitive are they? How much time can you spend with them? How much time have they spent with each other? Do they trust each other yet? Is there negative history they need to overcome? How well do their gifts fit together? Are the leaders working in their strengths? Are functions on the team working ineffectively because you don't yet have the right players on the team? Has the team gained enough wins to develop momentum?

A lot comes into play to develop a great team. That's why championship teams are so difficult to create and lead. But even if you don't make champions of your leaders, working to forge them into a team is worth the effort because of what it teaches them and how much more it develops them. It also helps you understand who the best leaders are, and they are the ones you will choose to develop further. That's the subject of the next chapter.

ACTION STEPS

1. Verify that your communication with your team of leaders is on point. Have you communicated to make sure team members are in alignment? If not, work on it. And as your team completes projects and initiatives, communicate praise by telling them how their work is making a difference. Make sure these bookends of communication are always in place.

2. Create bonding experiences for your team of leaders. Take them offsite for training and be sure to build in a time and place to connect and debrief. Plan leadership experiences for them where they are prompted to work together. Take the group out to dinner and talk about anything except work. The better they get to know and respect each other, the better they will be able to work together.

3. Schedule a group learning experience for the team. It can be as simple as asking everyone to read a book together and discuss it. The more the team grows together, the more valuable they become. And the shared experience also gives them common language and points of connection.

4. Perform a review of the placement of all the leaders in your team. Write a description of the position each person fills. Determine whether any necessary functions are currently unstaffed. Also look for redundancies in positions. Then write the strengths, weaknesses, and experience of the person who fills each position. Where are there

mismatches? How can you reposition team members to improve performance? Make those changes, helping team members understand why and how it will benefit the team.

ELEVEN

CHOOSE WHO TO DEVELOP FURTHER

M any years ago, when I was in the early part of my career, I decided to take some business courses in order to become a better leader in the area of finances. In one class, my economics professor taught something that changed my life: the Pareto principle, or what's commonly called the 80/20 rule. The idea was developed by Italian economist Vilfredo Pareto in the early twentieth century, when he observed a pattern that naturally occurred in nearly every aspect of life. It basically indicates that 20 percent of any group is responsible for 80 percent of its success in any given category.

- 20 percent of the workers produce 80 percent of the product
- 20 percent of the sales force close 80 percent of the sales
- 20 percent of the products return 80 percent of the revenue
- 20 percent of the population possesses 80 percent of the wealth
- 20 percent of the teams in a league win 80 percent of the championships

You get the idea. The actual statistics vary. They're not always exactly 20 and 80 percent, but they are usually pretty close. You can look at almost anything and find this pattern.

What's the significance of this? First, it goes against most people's instincts. We tend to assume things are going to be even. If five people are working on a team, we think they'll share the load evenly. They won't. If we need to raise $10,000 from a group of ten donors, we think, *If everybody gives $1,000, we'll have what we need.* But it never works that way. Some people will give nothing, and about $8,000 will usually come from just two people in the group.

When my professor explained this, it immediately made sense to me. I knew intuitively that the Pareto principle had the possibility of changing my life. I realized that *doing a few important things could give a much greater return than doing many less important things.* If I focused my efforts on the top 20 percent of my priorities, the Pareto principle meant I would receive an 80 percent return. I needed to become focused and intentional.

The Pareto Principle

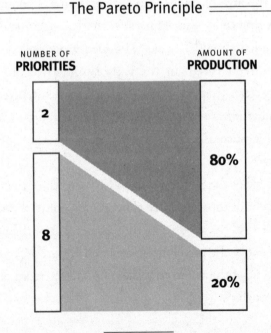

NUMBER OF
PRIORITIES

AMOUNT OF
PRODUCTION

2

8

80%

20%

I immediately started to apply the Pareto principle to how I worked. It transformed my productivity every day. It helped me confirm that I shouldn't just work hard and stay busy. If I had a to-do list with ten items on it, I didn't just start working on them. First, I ranked them in priority of importance or value, and then I devoted my time to the top two. That consistently gave me a high return on my work. Over and over, progress didn't come from how hard I worked; it came from how smart I worked.

I've used the Pareto principle for nearly fifty years, and it's helped me tremendously. While working on this book I came across an article by James Clear, the author of *Atomic Habits*, that dug into the Pareto principle. For example, Clear observed that in the NBA, 20 percent of franchises have won 75.3 percent of the championships, with the Boston Celtics and the Los Angeles Lakers having won nearly half of all the championships in NBA history. And in soccer, while seventy-seven different nations have competed in the World Cup, just three countries—Brazil, Germany, and Italy—won thirteen of the first twenty World Cup tournaments.

What fascinated me was how Clear took the 80/20 rule one step further. He described what he called the 1 Percent Rule: "The 1 Percent Rule states that over time the majority of the rewards in a given field will accumulate to the people, teams, and organizations that maintain a 1 percent advantage over the alternatives. You don't need to be twice as good to get twice the results. You just need to be slightly better."[1] Clear used an example from nature to describe how this works:

Imagine two plants growing side by side. Each day they will compete for sunlight and soil. If one plant can grow just a little bit faster than the other, then it can stretch taller, catch more sunlight, and soak up more rain. The next day, this additional energy allows the plant to grow even more. This pattern continues until the stronger plant crowds the other out and takes the lion's share of sunlight, soil, and nutrients.

From this advantageous position, the winning plant has a better ability to spread seeds and reproduce, which gives the species an even bigger footprint in the next generation. This process gets repeated again and again until the plants that are slightly better than the competition dominate the entire forest.

Scientists refer to this effect as "accumulative advantage." What begins as a small advantage gets bigger over time. One plant only needs a slight edge in the beginning to crowd out the competition and take over the entire forest. . . .

The margin between good and great is narrower than it seems. What begins as a slight edge over the competition compounds with each additional contest. . . .

Over time, those that are slightly better end up with the majority of the rewards.

> Accumulative advantage: "What begins as a small advantage gets bigger over time."
>
> —JAMES CLEAR

Clear said that while the Amazon rain forest contains more than 16,000 tree species, only 227 of those species make up more than 50 percent of forest.[2]

USE THE PARETO PRINCIPLE TO DEVELOP YOUR BEST

What does all this have to do with developing leaders? One of the greatest leadership discoveries I made in my life was that the Pareto principle could be applied to people. This was revolutionary to me. I had been trained and encouraged to love and value everyone, which is something I still strive to do every day. But that doesn't mean you're supposed to *develop* everyone! Compounding benefits will result from developing the top 20 percent.

Let's say you have ten people on your leadership team. Not everyone has the same potential. I'm sure you recognize that. The top two probably produce the majority of results for the team. Who do you think has the greatest *possibility* of producing the greatest return for your investment in them? The top two leaders. Why? Besides improving more quickly themselves, they can help others become more productive. If I have ten people on my leadership team, I focus my energy by investing 80 percent of my time and effort into my top two—my top 20 percent—by mentoring them. I add value to them, because they can multiply value to the others.

I started applying this principle to my teams forty years ago, and it transformed my leadership. Not only did it conserve my energy, because I was spending less time developing fewer leaders, but it multiplied my effectiveness because the leaders I chose gave me the highest return. It was multiplication by subtraction.

What about the others? you may be thinking. *Don't they deserve to be mentored? Are they just left out in the cold, getting nothing?* No, just because I don't mentor them doesn't mean they don't continue to get developed. They get the investment I put in my team of leaders. But guess what the top leaders I mentor are supposed to be doing? I expect them to develop the top leaders they influence. That includes the other members of my team. Everyone has the potential to be developed. The 9s on my leadership team should be developing 8s, the 7s should be developing 6s, the 5s developing 4s, and so on down the line.

Today everything I do is based on this idea. The companies I founded, the resources we develop, the books I write are all focused on adding value to leaders who multiply value to others. When I put my best effort into developing the best leaders and mentoring them to the next level—and they put their best effort into developing other leaders—everyone wins.

This development of the top 20 percent is the ultimate step in the development of leaders. This is what separates great teams from good ones. It separates teams that last from teams that flash in the pan. It enables teams and organizations to create successful succession plans. When you mentor your best leaders, it takes everything to another level.

As you prepare to choose who to develop further from your team of leaders, you need to be strategic, consistent, and intentional.

Be Strategic

When you choose leaders to invest in, you must stick to your top 20 percent—whether that means one leader out of five or ten leaders out of one hundred. Don't water down your selection to include people who aren't at that level yet. Let them rise up, and then select them. Remember, you have the potential to make an 80 percent impact if you choose your top 20 percent.

Be Consistent

One of the things I like about being older is that I've seen and done a lot in life, and that has given me perspective. I'm in my mid-seventies now, and I have observed the incredible compounding power of consistency. If you do the right things day in and day out, even though they may be small, they add up. It takes a long time for them to add up, but they *do* add up. Sometimes it's difficult for a young person to have the patience to do that. But as someone who has lived it, I can tell you that it's worth it.

Right Choices + Consistency + Time = Significant Returns

If you want to be a successful leader, the mentoring of your best leaders cannot be a one-and-done process. You can't select one group of people to mentor and expect to be finished. It needs to become a consistent practice month after month, year after year.

I'm living proof that consistency pays off. Here's a bit of my history:

In 1973 I understood that everything rises and falls on leadership. From that time forward, I invested daily in my personal growth and leadership development.

In 1976 I felt called to give my life to training leaders. Within weeks, I was training leaders, and I haven't stopped in more than forty years.

In 1979 I started writing books to help develop leaders. Since then, I've never stopped writing. To date, I've written more than one hundred books.

In 1984 I decided to develop resources to mentor leaders. That process started with the creation of a monthly audio lesson, and it has continued with seminars, videos, podcasts, digital learning systems, and coaching programs.

In 1986 I started my first company focused on leadership development. I've since founded three additional companies and two nonprofits, all focused on developing leaders, and they're still going strong.

In 1994 I began asking leaders to help me raise up more leaders. My first nonprofit organization, EQUIP, developed a strategy in which we recruited volunteer leaders who went overseas to train leaders. Those leaders they trained made a commitment to train more leaders themselves. We continue to use that leadership training model at home and abroad.

If you consistently invest in your own growth and development, and you consistently develop the top 20 percent of the leaders you have, it will change your leadership.

BE INTENTIONAL

I've always been an active person, but I wasn't always highly intentional. The events you just read from my personal history show how I become increasingly intentional in my development of leaders. I work to stay in my leadership lane by speaking, writing, and leading organizations whose purpose is to develop leaders.

Are you ready to become more intentional in your development of leaders? Are you willing to focus on mentoring the best leaders you have to become their best? If you are, then start thinking about who comprises your top 20 percent.

WHAT TO LOOK FOR IN LEADERS TO MENTOR

When you identified potential leaders and invited them to the leadership table, you had ideas about who might be a good leader. After developing them, empowering them to lead, and training them to work as a team, you now know what they can do. You've seen them in action. As you think about your experience with your leaders, look for these six characteristics to identify your best leaders.

1. A TRACK RECORD OF DEMONSTRATED LEADERSHIP

This may seem obvious, but I'm going to make the point anyway. When you're choosing your best leaders, you want people who have demonstrated their *leadership*, not just their *potential* to lead. Who has influenced others on your leadership team? When you put a bunch of leaders in a group together, an unofficial pecking order will quickly be established. Leaders intuitively know who the better leaders are. Who has risen to the top on your team when it comes to influence?

2. Understanding of Their Place and Purpose on the Team

The leaders you plan to further develop need to be self-aware enough to know their purpose and have a sense of what their best contribution is for the team. Building on their strengths is key to their development. Unfortunately, that kind of self-awareness is not always present in someone with high leadership capacity. Neither high capacity nor a successful track record is a surefire indicator that a leader will be self-aware. In talking to the top executive coaches who work for Maxwell Leadership, they've told me that poor self-awareness is the number one problem they see in leaders.

> In talking to the top executive coaches who work for Maxwell Leadership. they've told me that poor self-awareness is the number one problem they see in leaders.

If one of your best leaders doesn't know their strengths and weakness and isn't aware of how they can best contribute, you will have to decide if they're ready to be mentored. You may need to position them properly and help them develop self-awareness first. Tell them what you see in them. Point out their strengths. Give them roles that leverage those strengths and set expectations for them.

The whole process of mentoring needs to be based on your leaders' strengths. If they won't agree with what you believe they are, it will be difficult for you to develop them further.

3. Recognition of the Place and Purpose of Others

Never forget that there's a big difference between personal performance and effective leadership. Not all good *producers* can become good *leaders*. Leadership requires the leader to understand the team, recognize their strengths and weaknesses, know everyone's purpose, and know the best place for people on the team. They must demonstrate this ability not only with their followers, but also with other leaders. If they lack it, they won't hack it in higher leadership.

4. Willingness to Give Up Personal Agendas for the Vision

Talented people can get used to doing things their own way. This is especially true of talented leaders, because they possess influence and are accustomed to using it. But the leaders you intend to develop must demonstrate that they are willing to surrender their own agendas and adopt that of the team and organization to achieve the vision. They need to embrace the Law of Significance in *The 17 Indisputable Laws of Teamwork* which says: one is too small a number to achieve greatness.[3]

If they understand that as part of a team they can accomplish bigger and more significant things than they could on their own, then they deserve to be mentored and developed. You will be able to help them achieve a level of significance that outshines whatever perks, status, or opportunities individual success might offer. That can help them shift from thinking that they are *giving up* something by being part of the team to understanding that being on a team can *add up* to something greater. Individualism may win trophies, but a great team working together and sacrificing for one another can win championships.

5. Tangible Results in Their Leadership

I love what Coach Wooden used to say to his players: "Don't tell me what you are going to do. Show me." Talk can be cheap. Results are powerful. Any people on your leadership team who have great potential but haven't actually achieved results should be unproven. They are still *potential* leaders, not *proven* leaders. For you to heavily invest your time, energy, and resources mentoring people, they need to have proven themselves by leading team members to produce tangible results.

6. HUNGER TO GROW

One of the greatest enemies of effective leadership development is an arrival mind-set. If leaders believe they've "arrived," they will no longer work hard to produce. They won't roll up their sleeves every day to improve themselves and add value to the organization. They will no longer model the positive leadership values that got them there. As a result, they will eventually lose credibility and effectiveness. They will stop actively leading, because their focus will have shifted from seeking improvement to holding on to their place based on tenure, status, position, or history. When that happens, they are no longer teachable.

Whenever you invite leaders to be mentored, make it clear they haven't reached a *destination*. They're being given an *invitation*—to work just as hard, if not harder, but to make a greater impact doing it. By being mentored, they will gain greater influence and grow to make a larger contribution. They will be able to add more value to people because they will have more to give. And they will have the opportunity to make a greater impact for the organization. It's a start of something bigger. It's not the time to rest because they've been chosen. It's the time to make a major difference.

Choosing the right people to mentor is one of the most important tasks you can undertake as a leader. But it can also be the most difficult. Some leaders are easy to spot. Others aren't. Will you always get it right? If you're like me, the answer is no. In the past, I've chosen my share of the wrong people to develop. Some people lacked the character I thought they possessed and they crashed. Some were great talkers convincing me they had more potential than they actually did. Some didn't really want to grow. Others I thought I could help because I have a high belief in people, but they weren't capable. But none of those misses stopped me from continuing to develop and mentor leaders. I now consider those to be good misses. I'd rather occasionally make a wrong choice than miss the opportunity to invest in leaders.

WORK YOURSELF OUT OF A JOB

As you choose the best leaders to develop, I believe your ultimate goal should be to work yourself out of a job. That's the advice I always give leaders. Equip and develop leaders who replace you. It's what I've tried to do most of my life. I'm always looking around, asking, "Who can do what I am now doing?" For everything you do, there is almost always someone who can step into your shoes and take over.

Working yourself out of a job is the ultimate development win, and I recommend that you pursue it. Try to pass the baton in as many professional areas as you can. To accomplish that, do these three things:

1. Place a High Priority on Working Yourself Out of a Job

I haven't always been good at giving jobs to others. My tendency for many years was to pick up things that needing doing instead of passing them on to others. After a while, I was so loaded down doing things that I neglected the tasks that gave the highest return. If you can related, get out of that trap.

Begin by asking yourself, "What am I doing right now that could be done by someone else?" Once you've answered that, ask, "Who should I begin to develop to do this?"

2. PLACE A HIGHER PRIORITY ON DEVELOPING PEOPLE THAN PROTECTING YOUR POSITION

Most leaders are focused on holding the position they have or gaining the position they want. The focus is on themselves. Ironically, hoarding power is often what leads to someone losing power. The position doesn't make the leader; the leader makes the position. The way you expand your potential is to help others develop theirs. Raising up and equipping leaders makes you a better leader—and better able to do bigger and better things.

> The position doesn't make the leader; the leader makes the position.

3. PLACE A HIGHER PRIORITY ON SUCCESSION THAN ON SECURITY

Too many people in leadership positions are looking for security. But good leadership is never about holding fast. It's about moving forward. That's why I used to tell my staff, "Work yourself out of your job, and I'll give you another job." I wanted them to understand the truth of the adage, "A candle loses nothing by lighting another candle." Actually, there's more to it than that. I wanted them to learn that a candle *gains* something by lighting another candle— more light!

I believe that as a leader, if you work yourself out of a job, you'll always have another job. Success doesn't come from protecting what you have. It comes from developing others to replace you so that you can move on to bigger and better things. When you become a leader who develops leaders and mentors the best leaders you have, everybody rises. So choose the best leaders you have to further develop, and get ready to mentor them. I'll explain how in the next chapter.

ACTION STEPS

1. If you have never used the Pareto principle to help you become more personally productive, begin using it today. If you can maintain the discipline of focusing on the top 20 percent of your tasks and responsibilities on a day-to-day basis, you will experience its impact, making you more confident in using the principle to select leaders to develop.

2. Consider the leaders on your team. Rank each person on a scale of one (low) to ten (high) in the six characteristics mentioned in the chapter. Then tally their scores, rank them from highest to lowest, and identify your top 20 percent.

Leader	Track Record of Leadership	Self-Awareness of Place and Purpose	Recognition of Others' Place and Purpose	Willingness to Give Up Personal Agenda	Tangible Results of Leadership	Hunger to Grow	Total

As you look at the names of those top leaders, does your gut agree with your ranking? If not, why not? What other factors should come into play in your assessment? Who do you think could replace you in your current job if you moved on to bigger and better things? Reorder your list if needed. Once you're done, spend some more time reflecting on whether these are the leaders you should personally mentor. If you can get the advice of another leader, discuss your choices with them.

---

3. Think about the leaders you intend to develop and consider how many weeks, months, or years will be needed to mentor each of them. At this point, you will be making a guess. But you need to begin thinking about this because you will need to commit to being intentional and consistent over that period of time.

---

4. Set individual appointments with each of the leaders you intend to mentor to talk to them about it. However, don't meet with them until after you have read the next chapter. It has information you will need before you hold that first meeting.

TWELVE

MENTOR YOUR BEST LEADERS ONE-ON-ONE

Perhaps the greatest compliment you can give leaders is to offer to mentor them. But mentoring takes more than just skill. It takes finesse. It takes empathy. You need to be able to find common ground with those you mentor because your relationship must be able to go to another level of openness and authenticity. You must be open about your past failings and mistakes. And you must make the leader you're working with feel safe enough to be open and honest about where they're falling short and need to grow. Great mentors possess a spirit similar to that of singer-songwriter Carole King, who said, "I want to connect with people. I want people to think, 'Yeah, that's how I feel.'"[1] If you can do that, you have a much better chance of being able to develop leaders to the next level.

Soft skills, such as asking questions and listening, having empathy for people's journeys, and understanding their perspectives, are crucial in today's leadership environment. People won't automatically commit to you and your mentoring when *they* understand *you*. They'll commit to and follow you when they feel *understood*. I believe that will happen for you as a mentoring leader when you take the following actions:

- Value them
- Let them know you need them
- Include them in your journey
- Adopt a teachable spirit
- Ask questions
- Listen well and often
- Seek to know their perspective
- Give credit to them when they help you
- Express gratitude for those who helped you
- Replace *me* with *we*

> **"If you will sweat with your people, they can handle the heat."**

Years ago, a mentor told me, "If you will sweat with your people, they can handle the heat." I have found that to be true. When people understand that you're in it with them, they're more likely to engage with you.

HOW TO MENTOR LEADERS

If you've chosen leaders to mentor and you know that they are committed to you and a mentoring process, you're ready to begin. I want to give you a roadmap for how to mentor them. The map is simple, but the journey you take won't be. As a mentor, you need to be teacher, guide, coach, and cheerleader, and you must learn which to be at the appropriate time. But know this: there are few things that bring greater fulfillment in life. As you proceed, I recommend that you keep in mind these four things:

1. Choose Who You Mentor—Don't Let Them Choose You

Even though I've already discussed how to choose leaders to develop further, I want to emphasize this point because the more successful you become, the greater the number of people who will ask you for mentoring. You won't be able to mentor all of them. Nor should you. You should focus on helping the people of highest potential who are *a few steps* behind you, not the people who are *miles* behind you. Others are in a better position to mentor them.

It's crucial that *you* do the choosing. I learned this from the greatest leadership book I've ever read: the Bible. In fact, everything I know about leadership has its roots in the Bible. Jesus was an awesome leader. The Bible doesn't say that, but history proves it. No one mentored leaders more effectively than he did. He started with a small group of ordinary people, and those leaders created a worldwide movement.

Regi Campbell, an entrepreneur and author who founded Radical Mentoring, wrote about the importance of the selection process in mentoring using the Bible as an example:

Jesus picked the twelve. They didn't pick Him.

This is one of the most valuable lessons we take from Jesus. And one of the most countercultural aspects of becoming a mentor like Jesus.

Over and over I hear of young people seeking out mentors. "Could you have breakfast with me? I'd like to pick your brain if I could." We've all been there.

The Scriptures don't depict Jesus' mentoring that way. As a matter of fact, we can visualize the rich young ruler as he approached Jesus. He might have been saying, and I'm paraphrasing, "I've been cool. I've obeyed the commandments. What would it take for me to join up, to follow you, to become one of your inner circle?"

We can imagine Jesus . . . reading the young man's motives from his expression of interest in the kingdom: "Great, go sell all your possessions and come back to see me."

End of conversation.[2]

Letting others pick who you mentor would be like selecting your investments by agreeing to buy any fund from any salesperson who called to pitch it to you. There's no telling what you would end up with or what the outcome would be. Instead, you need to be selective about the people you agree to mentor. When you pick the right ones, you win, they win—everybody wins.

2. Set Expectations Up Front for Both of You

People enter mentoring relationships with all kinds of assumptions, and you know how the saying goes: assumptions are the mother of all mess ups! Charles Blair, another one of my early mentors, used to say, "Have an understanding so there is no misunderstanding." That's great advice as you enter a mentoring relationship with a leader. You need to lay the groundwork on everyone's part—the *we, you,* and *me* of the relationship. Here's how I set this up. When we sit down together for the first time, I go over the three sets of expectations:

"We" Expectations

I like to start with the things we both agree to do:

We will maintain an ROI agreement. Relationships don't last when they become one-sided. If that happens, the one doing all the giving starts to resent or regret the relationship. Mentoring is meant to give a return on investment to both people. When both people benefit, the relationship is life-giving. When they don't, somebody will soon want out of the relationship. Every time we meet, both of us need to feel that the experience was rewarding. If not, either of us can say it's run its course, and we can walk away at any time without blame or shame.

We will make each other better. Coming together with this sort of positive anticipation sets the tone for the experience. The person being mentored expects to be made better. But in the best relationships, the mentor gets better too. That requires both people to humbly bring something to the table. If they do, it becomes a wonderful growing experience. I recognize that there is more than one good way of seeing and doing things, so it's wise to expect everyone to be my teacher. You should too. That's the whole point of mentoring.

"You" Expectations

The next thing I want to do is let the person I will mentor know what I expect of him or her:

You must come ready. I like asking the people I mentor to set the agenda when we initially meet. I want them to tell me what their objectives are, what issues they are currently encountering, and what questions I can answer. I put the ball in their court. Then each time we meet, I ask them to send me their questions the day before we sit down together. That gives me a chance to think about my answers.

And I expect them to come to my location, be on time, be prepared, and engage at a deep level.

You must keep earning my time. My time is very limited, so I need to make the most of it. I'm sure that's true for you as well. Deciding to mentor someone is a choice I make, not an obligation I must fulfill. As long as the person I'm mentoring is making progress, I'm willing to keep meeting. If progress stops, so do I.

You must improve, not just learn. I expect the people I mentor to remain attentive, take notes, and learn. But engaging their intellect isn't enough. I want to see *change*. Applying what they learn by putting it into action is the only way for them to take charge of their growth and become leaders. That's why the first question I often ask in a mentoring meeting is how they applied what they learned the last time we met. It's a bad sign if they stammer or look like a deer in the headlights. However, more often than not, they tell me and then ask great follow-up questions. Deeper learning comes out of problems and from the application of lessons.

You must mentor other leaders. My whole reason for mentoring is to pass on what I learn. As I've said, my purpose is to add value to leaders who multiply value to others. I know of no better way to multiply value than for those I mentor to mentor others. The magic of mentoring is multiplication. When the young leaders I'm mentoring express a feeling of responsibility to help and develop others, I see that as maturity. It makes my day when someone I mentor introduces me to those they are mentoring. That's worth celebrating.

"Me" Expectations

Finally, I let the person I'm going to mentor know what he or she can expect from me and the standards I will uphold for myself:

I will be a safe person for you to share with. Good mentors are trustworthy and build a foundation of trust. Warren Bennis and Burt Nanus called trust "the glue that binds followers and leaders together."[3] Building trust may take time, but it's important because the depth of the mentoring will be determined by the vulnerability of the person being mentored. My part is to be real with mentees, allow every emotion I feel to show, be willing to answer any question, and hold everything they say in confidence. Trust is a result of authenticity, not perfection. Their part is to be real and open with me, not hide. They can expect me to be safe.

I will make myself available. Availability means you are dependable and accessible. When people need you, they can find you. The people I mentor know that I am as close as the phone. They have access to me. Seldom have people taken advantage of that access. They respect my time and only ask for it when it is essential. But I not only welcome their call to me, I also check in with them to make sure they're doing well. And I'm ready to jump in when they need my advice.

I will give you my best. My mentors always gave me their best. That impacted me. I am the fruit of their efforts. I may not be the best mentor, but the people I mentor will get my best effort. I work to live up to the standard that was set for me.

I will look out for your best interest. My mentoring advice will always be tailored to be what's best for the person I mentor. That does not mean we will always agree. That doesn't mean I'll give everyone whatever they ask for. It just means that I will do everything possible to keep my motives pure and put their interests first.

I've found that when I establish expectations up front, the mentoring relationship goes well. When I don't, it falls apart. I believe

> "Mentors do not seek to create a new person; they simply seek to help a person become a better version of himself."
>
> —JOHN WOODEN

you'll find the same thing to be true for you. In the end, as a mentor, you want to become a trusted friend. Even the great John Wooden wanted that for me. He never wanted to be my hero. He wanted the best for me. In his book on mentoring, he described the difference between heroes and mentors: "A hero is someone you idolize, while a mentor is someone you respect. A hero earns our amazement; a mentor earns our confidence. A hero takes our breath away; a mentor is given our trust. Mentors do not seek to create a new person; they simply seek to help a person become a better version of himself."[4] That's what you're going for.

3. PERSONALIZE YOUR MENTORING TO HELP LEADERS SUCCEED

One of my favorite things to do is communicate. I love engaging with people, taking them on an emotional journey, and teaching them things that will add value to them. But I always remember that's not mentoring. You can teach the masses, you can coach groups, but you have to mentor individuals one-on-one.

Leadership expert Peter Drucker said, "It is important to disciple a life, not teach a lesson." That's what mentoring is. It's discipling another person. It involves discerning where they are, knowing where they are supposed to go, and giving them what they need for the journey. Mentors must be good at evaluating people's potential and needs. They must be capable of understanding where people need to grow to reach the next level in their development. It's important to recognize, as Drucker said, that individuals are like flowers. One, like a rose, needs fertilizer. Another, like a rhododendron, doesn't. If you don't give flowers the care they need, they'll never bloom. Your first step in mentoring is to recognize who your people are and what they need individually.

As you mentor leaders, work to learn more about each person's personality type, learning style, love language, strengths, weaknesses, internal motivation, background, personal history, family relationships, aspirations, inspirations, and more. Leverage every bit of knowledge you have for every leader's benefit.

4. CARE ENOUGH TO HAVE CRUCIAL CONVERSATIONS

Good mentors don't hesitate to have difficult conversations with the people they mentor. They deal with the "elephants" in the room even when others won't. More often than not, the best time to have a crucial conversation is at the first opportunity. That's why I advise leaders to shovel the pile while it's small. However, if I think the conversation will be especially difficult for the other person, I sometimes say, "Let's talk about x the next time we meet," so that they have time to get prepared emotionally for such a talk. But I prefer not to wait.

> Good mentors don't hesitate to have difficult conversations with the people they mentor. They deal with the "elephants" in the room even when others won't.

The longer you put off having a difficult conversation, the more difficult it becomes because the timing feels increasingly awkward. Plus, silence communicates approval to most people. Furthermore, any problem that remains unaddressed typically snowballs and becomes more difficult to deal with later. And the longer you wait to talk about it, the less likely you are to address it. That would be poor mentoring.

In chapter 8, I mentioned Traci Morrow. For the last several years, I've spent time mentoring her, and we've had quite a few crucial conversations. Recently, I asked her if she would feel comfortable sharing about our conversations, and she was more than willing. Here is what she said:

> I can count on you to tell me the truth. Typically, you deliver truth wrapped in a question, and always with a choice—my choice—and having options leaves me feeling valued by you. One of the first things you did as our mentoring relationship began was ask me my love language, and when you found out it was words of affirmation, you made sure to speak my language. But that's not just to say you only give me words of praise and appreciation, though you certainly do. What I most value is that you speak words that help me grow, the hard words many people aren't blessed enough to hear from a beloved, trusted mentor.
>
> You have challenged me on a few occasions to make a decision when I was hesitant, and to make a hard call that I'd put off or wasn't addressing. You've challenged me when I've been passive when I needed to take action and have shared hard truths in the most loving manner I've ever received outside of a parent or my husband. I am amazed that somehow you share insight with me that draws out my best rather than shutting me down. Your words call forth my inner tenacious leader rather than making me feel small.
>
> One of our sessions really stands out. It was after I did an interview with someone in a public arena, and I lost my connection with the audience. It just fell flat. I knew something was off about halfway through, but I was too close to see what I was missing. I could not wait to get your feedback. For most people that would be scary to hear feedback from a master communicator on a job not done well, but for me, I'd already felt the worst of it; I'd suffered through the interview. I wanted to dissect my performance to see where it broke down, and because I know you desire to help me, you'd give it to me straight.

As you walked through my errors, you spoke in a kind voice and without sugarcoating your feedback. I was learning two things that day: how to not lose connection with an audience, but also how to mentor someone when they've just had a failure.

I always leave my conversations with you knowing what I need to do to grow and feeling the freedom to really choose growth. I can see in your face and hear in your voice that you believe in my ability to do what's necessary to grow. It's not fun to hear hard truths, but somehow, I look forward to your feedback. The root of that is trust.

That's the kind of feedback every mentor cherishes. I believe in Traci's potential and want what's best for her. That's the way I feel about everyone I mentor. They're like my daughters and sons, so I want to bring out the best in them and see them become their best. The only way to do that is to be willing to say the hard things that will help them.

When you engage in a crucial conversation, you need to be willing to tell the other person what she needs to hear—for her benefit, not yours. Yes, you should express it in a way that will be best received by the person. But the message needs to really help them. Sometimes a mentor is the only truth teller in a leader's life.

There's one more important thing I need to say about crucial conversations with leaders you mentor. They should be a two-way street. As a mentor, you need to be just as open to hearing the truth as the person you mentor. That's why I give all my leaders permission to speak into my life. I want them to be able to have crucial conversations with me when they see that I need it.

My friend Ed Bastian, the CEO of Delta, has the same attitude. He says to his inner circle: "Tell me what I should stop doing . . . keep doing . . . and start doing." That's exceptional coming from the leader of one of the world's largest companies.

The mentoring process looks different for every mentor and for every leader who is being mentored. That's how it should be. It's a very personal experience. But the result should be the same. The leader being mentored should move up to a higher level of leadership. The ultimate step in mentoring ends with the leader being mentored taking the baton from his mentor and surpassing him.

I came across a touching story that illustrates this concept. It may be apocryphal, but I love it just the same:

> It's told of Leonardo da Vinci that while still a pupil, before his genius burst into brilliancy, he received a special inspiration in this way: His old and famous master, because of his growing infirmities of age, felt obliged to give up his own work, and one day bade da Vinci finish for him a picture which he had begun. The young man had such reverence for his master's skill that he shrank from the task. The old artist, however, would not accept any excuse, but persisted in his command, saying simply, "Do your best."
>
> Da Vinci at last trembling seized the brush and, kneeling before the easel, prayed: "It is for the sake of my beloved master that I implore skill and power for this undertaking." As he proceeded his hand grew steady, his eye awoke with slumbering genius. He forgot himself and was filled with enthusiasm for his work. When the painting was finished the old master was carried into the studio to pass judgment on the result. His eye rested on a triumph of art. Throwing his arms around the young artist, he exclaimed, "My son, I paint no more."[5]

That is what a great mentor ultimately wants to see. He wants to pour himself into his student, and see his student surpass him. It is the picture of a mentoring masterpiece. We may never achieve it, but we should never stop striving.

ACTION STEPS

1. Once you have invited a leader to be mentored and they agree, set an appointment to meet. Before you do, write out your expectations using the "we, you, me" method.

   _____

2. When you meet, go over the expectations you have of the leader you intend to mentor. In addition, ask them to express their expectations. If you come to agreement, plan your next meeting, explaining that you want your mentee to come with specific questions for you.

   _____

3. Each time you meet, answer your mentee's questions. As you notice issues, problems, or deficits in the person, address them. Ask questions. Explain what you have observed. Offer advice or resources to help them. Give assignments. And schedule your next meeting. Determine a good rhythm for the frequency of your meetings.

   _____

4. As long as you see progress in the leader you're mentoring, agree to keep meeting. When the leader stops growing, doesn't follow through with assignments, or stops asking good questions, discuss whether the relationship has run its course. If it has, stop scheduling regular meetings. You can always leave the door open to future connection if the leader needs it.

   _____

THIRTEEN

TEACH YOUR LEADERS TO DEVELOP OTHER LEADERS

If you have used the guidelines in this book to train, develop, and mentor leaders, you have already put yourself in rare company. The majority of leaders content themselves with gathering and leading followers; few put in the effort to develop people to become effective leaders. Congratulations! I want to praise you and encourage you to keep developing others. But I also want to tell you there's still one step higher you can climb as a leader. You can teach your leaders to follow in your footsteps and become developers of leaders in their own right. And that's a worthy goal, because Every organization needs more and better leaders. The only thing limiting the future of any organization is the number of good leaders it develops.

> The only thing limiting the future of any organization is the number of good leaders it develops.

The greater the number of people with

outstanding leadership ability, the greater the potential success of an organization. That's one of the reasons I teach the Law of the Bench in *The 17 Indisputable Laws of Teamwork*: great teams have great depth.[1] Why?

- A good bench gives a team expanded capacity.
- A good bench gives a team greater flexibility.
- A good bench gives a team long-term sustainability.
- A good bench gives a team multiple options.

And when that team is populated with good leaders, all those advantages are multiplied.

When I led my first organization, I didn't initially understand the importance of teaching others to develop leaders. But I eventually recognized the concept of *reproducing* leaders when I understood something in the Bible written by the Apostle Paul, who was a world-class leader. In a letter to Timothy, a young man he was mentoring. Paul told him, "Pass on what you heard from me . . . to reliable leaders who are competent to teach others."[2]

Don't worry: you don't have to be a person of faith to learn from this lesson. Here's what you need to understand. Paul had equipped, developed, and personally mentored Timothy to become a leader. In this letter to Timothy, Paul was teaching him to take that final step in his development: to become a leader who developed leaders himself.

That passage changed my focus and gave me a new goal: developing leaders who reproduced leaders. For fifty years my vision has been to reproduce leaders who will continue that process with others. Once I started investing in people with high potential, I never stopped. And after I became competent at developing leaders, I worked on emulating Paul, whose vision was to develop leaders who reproduced other leaders. You can embrace that same goal.

DON'T STOP GIVING

There's a very real temptation for leaders who achieve a level of success to rest on their laurels. The climb to leadership can be strenuous, and some people want to enjoy the view from the top. They want to stop and smell the roses. But that's not the best purpose of leadership achievement. The best purpose is to use everything you've learned to give a hand up to others, helping them become leaders, and then teaching them to do the same for others with potential.

One of the leaders who helped me and many others to develop was author and pastor Jack Hayford. Jack used to say the secret sauce to success is this: *make decisions against yourself.* Author Mark Batterson, who also learned important lessons from Jack, commented on this, saying

> We want success without sacrifice, but life doesn't work that way. Success will not be shortchanged. You have to pay the price, and it never goes on sale. The best decision you can make for yourself is making decisions against yourself. You have to discipline yourself to do the right things day in and day out, week in and week out, year in and year out. And if you do, the payoff is far greater than the price you paid. . . .
>
> Now let's bring this idea down to earth for you. If you want to get out of debt, you've got to make decisions against yourself financially. It's called sticking to a budget. If you want to get into shape, you've got to make decisions against yourself physically. Join the gym.[3]

Jack's secret sauce applies to leadership development. If you want a successful organization with more and better leaders, you need to pay the price. You need to make the decision against yourself of resting on your laurels or enjoying your success, and instead invest your time in developing leaders who reproduce themselves.

I believe there are seven different growth levels that you must achieve to become a reproducing leader:

1. Growth that makes you capable of doing your job well
2. Growth that enables you to grow others in your job
3. Growth that allows you to reproduce yourself in your job
4. Growth that provides opportunities for higher-level leadership
5. Growth that prepares you to develop others to higher levels of leadership
6. Growth that stretches you enough to have a mentoring relationship with growing leaders
7. Growth that gives you the ability to develop leaders who reproduce leaders

If you want to reach your full leadership potential, then you need to develop leaders who carry the same vision for developed people into leaders to reach their potential. If you do that and they do that, the leadership pipeline you create will never run dry.

DEVELOPING A REPRODUCING ENVIRONMENT

If you want to move up those growth levels—and encourage other leaders on your team or within your organization to do the same—you need to create an environment that promotes leadership reproduction. To accomplish this, you need to have these five expectations in place and ensure that they are met by the people you lead:

1. The Leader of the Team Models Leadership Development

What happens on your team starts with you. If you want leaders to develop other leaders, you must continue to model it, nurture it, monitor it, and incentivize it. In the midst of all your other responsibilities, you must make the development of leaders your highest priority. In chapter 7, I mentioned Mark Miller, Chick-fil-A's vice president of high-performance leadership. He said, "We believe leadership can become our primary competitive advantage. We want to become known as an organization that can proudly and confidently say, 'Leaders Made Here.'"[4] I love that statement. Every organization that wants to create a leadership environment should adopt it.

As I work to lead organizations that focus on leadership development, I strive to model the six Cs of an environment where leaders reproduce other leaders:

- **Character—be it.** Everything starts with strong character. That's not something you can just talk about; it's something that must be at the core of who you are. You have to live it every day. You must maintain integrity, treat others with respect, desire the best for people, and go out of your way to help them.

- **Clarity—show it.** You must spend time developing leaders yourself. You need to be personally involved, and your team needs to see you doing it so that they understand how it's done and how important it is.

- **Communication—say it.** You need to constantly talk about leadership development, so it becomes part of the common language and everyday conversation.

- **Contribution—own it.** If you're the leader, the buck stops with you. You need to own your responsibility for developing leaders. Do that and others will too.

- **Consistency—do it.** The development of leaders is never one and done. It's something that needs cultivating every day. Why? Because the need for more and better leaders never ends.
- **Celebration—practice it.** When the development of leaders is recognized, rewarded, and celebrated continually, it becomes elevated in the organization and woven into the culture. Every leader aspires to become part of it and join in.

> "Nothing is easier than saying words. Nothing is harder than living them, day after day. What you promise today must be renewed and re-decided tomorrow and each day that stretches out before you."
>
> —ARTHUR GORDON

Arthur Gordon said, "Nothing is easier than saying words. Nothing is harder than living them, day after day. What you promise today must be renewed and re-decided tomorrow and each day that stretches out before you."[5] When the leader models leadership development daily, everyone on the team recognizes its importance. If the leader neglects it or delegates it to someone else, it sends the message that it's not a high priority.

2. Everyone Is Expected to Develop Someone

An organization where leaders are continually being developed is modeled from the top, but it's grown from the bottom up. What does that mean? It looks like this:

- Everyone has someone developing or mentoring them.
- Everyone shares their experiences developing and mentoring others.
- Everyone has someone to develop or mentor.

There is an intentionality in a reproductive environment meant to create a mentoring movement. Teaching and learning are normal and expected, and nobody is required be a leader to do it. *Everyone* is involved. People are continually learning from each other. Everyone is sharing experiences. Growth is normal and expected.

Developing this kind of environment requires people to challenge one another to get out of their comfort zones. A great way to do that is to ask challenging questions. In *Starting Strong*, authors Lois J. Zachary and Lory A. Fischler listed good questions that can be used to challenge people to grow:

- When was the last time you pushed yourself out of your comfort zone?
- What would it take to get you out of your comfort zone?
- What is something you've been afraid to try that would challenge you?
- What additional knowledge, skill, or experience are you lacking?
- What can I do to support you as you're learning right now?[6]

The bottom line is that taking on the role of developer must become a mind-set, as I discussed in chapter 1. For it to grow, it must be adopted by everyone. When it does, the organization shifts and its potential expands.

3. Leaders Focus on Developing Leaders, Not Recruiting More Followers

It's often easy for a talented leader to attract and recruit followers, especially if that leader has high charisma or possesses a compelling vision. But the future of an organization depends on the development of more and better leaders, not the recruitment of more and better followers.

Leaders who focus on recruiting followers are actually shrinking their organization, not expanding it. I read a story in *The New Dynamics of Winning* by Denis Waitley that provides a fantastic visual image of this shrinking effect:

> David Ogilvy, founder of the giant advertising agency Ogilvy and Mather, used to give each new manager in his organization a Russian doll. The doll contained five progressively smaller dolls. A message inside the smallest one read: "If each of us hires people who are smaller than we are, we shall become a company of dwarfs. But if each of us hires people who are bigger than we are, Ogilvy and Mather will become a company of giants." Commit to finding, hiring, and developing giants.[7]

Maybe you've seen one of these nesting Russian dolls, called a *matryoshka*. They're sold everywhere in Russia. Some are very elaborate and have a dozen or more progressively smaller dolls one inside the other. When leaders focus on recruiting followers—and those followers also recruit others who will follow them—it shrinks down the leadership "size" of the organization. However, when leaders focus on developing others to their highest capability, it enlarges the leadership size and potential of the organization.

Noel Tichy, author of *The Leadership Engine*, said, "Winning companies win because they have good leaders who nurture the development of other leaders at all levels of the

> "Winning companies win because they have good leaders who nurture the development of other leaders at all levels of the organization."
>
> —NOEL TICHY

organization."[8] It's vital to understand that it takes a leader to reproduce another leader. A nonleader cannot develop a leader. Neither can an institution. It takes a leader to know one, show one, and grow one.

4. PEOPLE ARE CONTINUALLY GROWING THEMSELVES OUT OF THEIR JOBS

In chapter 11, I described how good leaders work themselves out of a job. One of the key transitions to becoming a reproducer of leaders is to focus less on what you can accomplish personally and more on what you can accomplish through others.

Leaders who work in a reproducing environment grow themselves out of jobs continually. Every time they assume a new role or are put in a new position, as soon as they've mastered the job, they begin equipping someone to replace themselves. The best leaders also develop their replacements in leadership.

Speaker Philip Nation described this process:

As leaders, we are in the business of replacing ourselves. It would be easy to make the case that if you are not preparing someone else to take your place and/or outpace your abilities, then you are not truly leading people. Often, the desire to stay in the position of leadership comes from a "command and control" attitude. It is the kind of leadership found in *The Prince* by Machiavelli. It is a leadership that enlists people into your work but never releases them for any other work.[9]

When leaders repeatedly grow themselves out of a job by developing someone to replace them, they expand their capabilities, and they free themselves to do bigger and better things in the organization. That not only allows them to move up, but it also makes room for others to rise up behind them.

I like how this occurs in the NFL. Successful teams have reproduction cultures. You can see it in how teams look for players with leadership ability, not just football talent, in the draft and free agency. You see it in the way veteran players are expected to mentor and develop younger players. And it's especially obvious in the way the best coaches develop their coordinators and assistants not only to succeed in their current jobs, but to be ready to step up to their next level of leadership. If you were to look at most of the great head coaches in the NFL, you could trace their preparation back to other coaches who developed them. The chain of leadership development often goes back many generations, spanning many dozens of years.

How can you measure how well people are growing themselves out of their jobs? Ask the following questions about each of your leaders:

- Are there more followers than leaders on this person's team?
- Is this leader doing the exact same job year after year?
- Is this leader working long hours?
- Is this leader carrying the load by himself?

If the answer is yes to these questions, then your leaders are not growing themselves out of their jobs. And they're not helping the organization develop leaders for the future. You need to meet with them and help them figure out why they're stuck.

5. Leaders Become More than Mentors—They Become Sponsors

When I talked to Sheri Riley so that I could write about her story in chapter 2, she explained the difference between an advisor, a mentor, and a sponsor. She said that an advisor speaks on your behalf. She is an advocate. A mentor helps and guides you by pouring into you. But a sponsor opens doors for you so that you can walk through them to be successful. Essentially, a sponsor says, "Here's the opportunity," and gives the new leader the chance to show up and take it.

Economist Sylvia Ann Hewlett, founder of the Center for Talent Innovation, has written about the value of having a sponsor:

> Who's pulling for you? Who's got your back? Who's putting your hat in the ring?
>
> Odds are, this person is not a mentor but a sponsor.
>
> Now don't get me wrong: mentors matter. You absolutely need them—they give valuable advice, build self-esteem, and provide an indispensable sounding board when you're unsure about next steps. But they are not your ticket to the top.
>
> If you're interested in fast-tracking your career, in getting that next hot assignment or making more money, what you need is a sponsor. Sponsors give advice and guidance, but they also come through on much more important fronts. In particular they:
>
> > Believe in your value and your potential and are prepared to link reputations and go out on a limb on your behalf.
> >
> > Have a voice at decision-making tables and are willing to be your champion—convincing others that you deserve a pay raise or a promotion.
> >
> > Are willing to give you air cover so that you can take risks. No one can accomplish great things in this world if they don't have a senior leader in their corner making it safe to fail.[10]

Sponsors take an active role in making the leaders they're developing successful. Tom Phillippe was a sponsor to me when I was in my early thirties. He saw my potential and opened doors for me to walk through to achieve success. When I needed an introduction, he gave it to me. When I failed, he helped me get back up. When others criticized me, he defended me. When I succeeded, he cheered me on. When I did something stupid, he protected me. When I needed to develop maturity, he was patient with me. He walked before me to help clear my path. He walked beside me and encouraged my every step. He walked behind me to serve me. He often aided me with his presence, and he always supported me with his heart.

Even after I started to become more successful, he continued to advocate for me. He was my sponsor for forty years. I traveled farther and climbed higher because of him. Tom spoke potential into my life, and backed it up by putting himself on the line for me. I'll always be grateful for him. He died in 2018 at age eighty-nine. I still miss him.

As you seek to be a reproducing leader, become a sponsor. Equipping someone to do a job is fantastic, but don't just equip people. Developing someone to become a leader is great, but don't just develop people. Mentoring someone to become a high-level leader is tremendous, but don't just mentor people. Become a sponsor. Open doors for them. Advocate for them. Put yourself on the line to help them to reach their highest potential. Pave the way for their success, and if they surpass you, become their biggest cheerleader.

A GREAT LEADERSHIP ROI

One of my favorite success stories illustrating the compounding return of developing leaders comes from Kevin Myers, the leader of 12Stone Church. When I moved to Atlanta in 1997, I started mentoring Kevin one on one. I'd met Kevin and his wife, Marcia, soon after they graduated from college. When I chose to mentor him, he was already an excellent communicator and a good leader. His organization was growing, and he was hungry to learn. Kevin says, "When you hang around people at your level, you feel pretty good about your game and start to think you have more answers than questions. But as soon as you're around people in the league of play ahead of you, you realize the gap is greater and you have more questions than answers."

When it comes to leadership development. Kevin has been like a river, not a reservoir. Whatever I have poured into him, he has continually poured out to others. He doesn't receive it just for his own benefit; he blesses others, giving them his best. He's grown 12Stone tremendously, from an attendance of 800 to more than 10,000. But much of his focus has been on developing leaders, first on his staff, and then in a residency program he created, modeled after the training doctors receive after they graduate from medical school.

So 12Stone has developed 300 leaders in their residency program, and another 300 leaders in other churches who have adopted their program. In addition, Kevin and members of his executive team, such as my friend Dan Reiland, the executive director of leadership expansion at the Maxwell Leadership Center, continually invest in hundreds of other leaders and coach them regularly.

Everything I have poured into Kevin to develop him has compounded. And the way he is living and leading, everything he is pouring into other leaders is compounding. It's one of the most rewarding things I've experienced as a leader. Little did I know when I began developing leaders that it would give me such an incredible return. I didn't do it for that reason. I developed leaders for what they could bring to others. That is still my motive for mentoring others.

And what's wonderful is that you can have a similar experience. By developing leaders who reproduce other leaders, you can create a leadership-intensive organization with a great bench of current and future leaders. You can create a leadership pipeline that that never runs dry, that never runs out of leaders and is set up to go after new and greater opportunities.

Teaching your leaders to create other leaders is the last step in a long journey of developing leaders. But the journey shouldn't end there. Why do I say that? Because in a positive, healthy, successful, growing organization, the process of developing leaders never stops. The best leaders continue to invest in people like their future depends on it— because it does.

The good news is you can invest in others and develop leaders. You can experience the personal and professional rewards that the process brings. Will it be challenging? Yes. Will it take a long time to achieve? You know it. Will you make mistakes? Undoubtedly. But will it be worth it? Absolutely! No matter what it costs you, the return you receive will eclipse the price. Developing leaders is the most organizationally valuable action you can take.

And as a result, while other organizations are still trying to figure out what's next, your leaders will be out conquering new territory. While others are scrambling to find someone to champion their next initiative, you'll be taking your pick of leaders from your deep bench. When developing leaders becomes a lifestyle for everyone in your organization, you can't help but be successful. And you will have positioned yourself and your organization to receive the highest return that comes from developing leaders: compounding. The rewards continue to grow, and the return actually *increases* over time.

If you want a better team, a better organization, and a better future personally and professionally, dedicate yourself to developing leaders. It will be one of the most impacting and rewarding things you ever do.

ACTION STEPS

1. Make sure the value of developing more leaders rather than gathering more followers is championed on your team or in your organization. Model it, communicate it, and expect it of everyone you lead.

   _____

2. Talk to all your leaders and ask them who they are developing. Get names, and ask where those people are in the process, and ask the leaders what they are doing specifically to develop or mentor them. If you discover that the same person is being mentored by multiple leaders, ask some of those leaders to take on new mentees. Challenge leaders who are not actively developing or mentoring people to select someone immediately and start the process.

   _____

3. Who on your team has worked themselves out of a job? If the answer is no one, you have not yet succeeded in developing an environment of leadership reproduction. Give leaders incentives for reproducing themselves, and when they do, reward them by elevating them to new responsibilities.

   _____

4. Elevate sponsorship in your organization. Model it with the leaders you're developing and mentoring. Communicate its value to your leaders. And reward people who sponsor new leaders. What gets rewarded is what gets done.

   _____

ABOUT THE AUTHOR

John C. Maxwell is a #1 *New York Times* bestselling author, speaker, coach and leader who has sold more than 34 million books in fifty languages. He is the founder of Maxwell Leadership®—the leadership development organization created to expand the reach of his principles of helping people lead powerful, positive change. Maxwell's books and programs have been translated into 70 languages and have been used to train tens of millions of leaders in every nation. His work also includes that of the Maxwell Leadership Foundation and EQUIP, nonprofit organizations that have impacted millions of adults and youth across the globe through values-based, people-centric leadership training.

John has been recognized as the #1 leader in business by the American Management Association and as the world's most influential leadership expert by both *Business Insider* and *Inc.* magazines. He is a recipient of the Horatio Alger Award and the Mother Teresa Prize for Global Peace and Leadership from the Luminary Leadership Network.

Maxwell and the work of Maxwell Leadership continue to influence individuals and organizations worldwide—from Fortune 500 CEOs and national leaders to entrepreneurs and the leaders of tomorrow. For more information about him and Maxwell Leadership, visit maxwellleadership.com.

Notes

Chapter 1: Understand the Answer

1. Jazmine Boatman and Richard S. Wellins, *Time for a Leadership Revolution: Global Leadership Forecast 2011* (Pittsburgh: Development Dimensions International, 2011), 8, https://www.ddiworld.com/DDI /media/trend-research/globalleadershipforecast2011_globalreport_ddi.pdf.
2. Maxwell, *The 21 Irrefutable Laws of Leadership*, 167 (see intro, n. 4).
3. Michael McQueen, *Momentum: How to Build It, Keep It or Get It Back* (Melbourne: Wiley Australia, 2016), 7–9.
4. Dave Anderson, *Up Your Business! 7 Steps to Fix, Build, or Stretch Your Organization*, 2nd ed. (Hoboken, NJ: John Wiley and Sons, 2007), loc. 3284 of 4786, Kindle.
5. Quoted in Michael D. Ames, *Pathways to Success: Today's Business Leaders Tell How to Excel in Work, Career, and Leadership Roles* (San Francisco: Berrett-Koehler, 1994), 175.
6. A. L. Williams, *All You Can Do Is All You Can Do but All You Can Do Is Enough!* (New York: Ivy, 1989), 133.
7. Gayle D. Beebe, *The Shaping of an Effective Leader: Eight Formative Principles of Leadership* (Downers Grove, IL: InterVarsity Press, 2011), 22.
8. "Carnegie's Epitaph," *Los Angeles Herald*, 29, no. 132, February 10, 1902, https://cdnc.ucr.edu/cgi-bin/cdnc?a=d&d=LAH19020210.2.88&e =--------en--20--1--txt-txIN--------1.
9. The Inspiring Journal, "50 Powerful and Memorable Zig Ziglar Quotes," *The Inspiring Journal* (blog), May 7, 2015, https://www. theinspiringjournal.com/50-powerful-and-memorable-zig-ziglar-quotes/.

Chapter 2: Commit to Developing People

1. John Wooden and Don Yaeger, *A Game Plan for Life: The Power of Mentoring* (New York: Bloomsbury, 2009), 4.
2. Dale Carnegie Bronner, *Pass the Baton!: The Miracle of Mentoring* (Austell, GA: Carnegie, 2006), loc. 128 of 1071, Kindle.
3. Ryan B. Patrick, "Usher: Underrated," *Exclaim!*, September 14, 2016, http://exclaim.ca/music/article/usher-underrated.
4. Gary Trust, "Chart Beat Thursday: Usher, will.i.am, B.o.B," *Billboard*, May 6, 2010, https://www.billboard.com/articles/columns/chart-beat /958333/chart-beat-thursday-usher-william-bob.
5. Usher Raymond IV, foreword to *Exponential Living: Stop Spending 100% of Your Time on 10% of Who You Are*, by Sheri Riley (New York: New American Library, 2017), xii.

Chapter 3: Get to Know Them

1. Gregory Kesler, "How Coke's CEO Aligned Strategy and People to Re-Charge Growth: An Interview with Neville Isdell," *Journal of the Human Resource Planning Society* 31, no. 2 (2008): 18.
2. Neville Isdell with David Beasley, *Inside Coca-Cola: A CEO's Life Story of Building the World's Most Popular Brand* (New York: St. Martin's, 2011), loc. 3 of 254, Kindle.
3. Isdell, *Inside Coca-Cola*, loc. 5 of 254.
4. Kesler, "How Coke's CEO Aligned Strategy and People to Re-Charge Growth," 19.
5. Kesler, "How Coke's CEO Aligned Strategy and People to Re-Charge Growth," 20.
6. Isdell, *Inside Coca-Cola*, loc. 179 of 254.
7. Steven B. Sample, *The Contrarian's Guide to Leadership* (San Francisco: Jossey-Bass, 2002), 21.
8. Quoted in Bruce Larson, *My Creator, My Friend: The Genesis of a Relationship* (Waco, Texas: Word, 1986), 166.
9. Herb Cohen, *You Can Negotiate Anything: The World's Best Negotiator Tells You How to Get What You Want*, reissue ed. (New York: Bantam, 1982), 217.
10. "Larry King in quotes," *The Telegraph*, December 16, 2010, https://www .telegraph.co.uk/culture/tvandradio/8207302/Larry-King-in-quotes.html.

11. David W. Augsburger, *Caring Enough to Hear and Be Heard* (Harrisonburg, VA: Herald Press, 1982), 12.
12. Simon Sinek, *Start with Why: How Great Leaders Inspire Everyone to Take Action* (New York: Portfolio, 2009), 11–12.
13. Steffan Surdek, "Why Understanding Other Perspectives Is a Key Leadership Skill," *Forbes*, November 17, 2016, https://www.forbes.com /sites/forbescoachescouncil/2016/11/17/why-understanding-other -perspectives-is-a-key-leadership-skill/#7496edae6d20.

Chapter 4: Equip Your Team

1. Steve Olenski, "8 Key Tactics for Developing Employees," *Forbes*, July 20, 2015, https://www.forbes.com/sites/steveolenski/2015/07/20/8-key-tactics -for-developing-employees/#4ec359f56373.
2. Quoted in Ken Shelton, *Empowering Business Resources: Executive Excellence on Productivity* (n.p.: Scott, Foresman, 1990), 100.
3. James Donovan, "How a 70/20/10 Approach to Training Can Positively Impact Your Training Strategy," *Commscope Training* (blog), September 27, 2017, https://blog.commscopetraining.com/702010-learning-development -philosophy-fits-infrastructure-industry/.
4. Olenski, "8 Key Tactics for Developing Employees."

Chapter 5: Identify Potential Leaders

1. James M. Kouzes and Barry Z. Posner, foreword to *The Hidden Leader: Discover and Develop the Greatness Within Your Company*, by Scott K. Edinger and Laurie Sain (New York: AMACOM, 2015), loc. 136 of 366, Kindle.
2. Lorin Woolfe, *The Bible on Leadership: From Moses to Matthew—Management Lessons for Contemporary Leaders* (New York: AMACOM, 2002), 207.
3. William D. Cohan, "How One of the Country's Most Stories C.E.O.s Destroyed His Legacy," *New York Times*, November 21, 2022, https:// www.nytimes.com/2022/11/21/opinion/jack-welch-ge-jeff-immelt.html ?algo=combo_als_clicks_decay_96_50_ranks&fellback=false&imp _id=506927408&pool=pool%2F87cbbdd5-1c6c-4d21-8300-fc2c052afff3 &req_id=46232210&surface=for-you-email-rotating-profile&variant =0_best_algo&nl=for-you&emc=edit_fory_20221124&nlid=59190517& block=5&rank=2.

4. Quoted in Eric Buehrer, *Charting Your Family's Course* (Wheaton, IL: Victor, 1994), 110.

5. Ed Bastian (CEO of Delta Airlines), in conversation with the author.

6. Jeffrey Cohn and Jay Morgan, *Why Are We Bad at Picking Good Leaders?* (San Francisco: Jossey-Bass, 2011), 47.

7. Carol Loomis, *Tap Dancing to Work: Warren Buffett on Practically Everything, 1966–2013* (2012; repr., New York: Portfolio, 2013), 135.

8. James A. Cress, "Pastor's Pastor: I'm Glad They Said That!" *Ministry*, December 1997, https://www.ministrymagazine.org/archive/1997/12 /im-glad-they-said-that.

9. Beebe, *The Shaping of an Effective Leader*, 30 (see intro, n. 2).

10. Bastian, conversation with author.

11. Ralph Waldo Emerson, *Essays & Lectures*, ed. Joel Porte (n.p.: Library of America, 1983), 310.

12. Aleksandr Solzhenitsyn, *The First Circle*, trans. Thomas P. Whitney (London: Collins, 1968), 3.

13. John C. Maxwell, *The 15 Invaluable Laws of Growth: Live Them and Reach Your Potential* (2012; repr., New York: Center Street, 2014), chap. 10.

14. "Mario Andretti: Inducted 2005," Automotive Hall of Fame, accessed May 28, 2019, https://www.automotivehalloffame.org/honoree/mario -andretti/.

15. Red Auerbach with Ken Dooley, MBA: *Management by Auerbach: Management Tips from the Leader of One of America's Most Successful Organizations* (New York: Macmillan, 1991), 28.

16. Maxwell, *The 21 Irrefutable Laws of Leadership*, 169 (see intro, n. 4).

17. Maxwell, 73.

18. David Walker, "After Giving 1,000 Interviews, I Found the 4 Questions That Actually Matter," *Inc.*, June 23, 2017, https://www.inc.com/david -walker/after-giving-1000-interviews-i-found-the-4-questions-that -actually-matter.html.

19. John C. Maxwell, *Leadershift: The 11 Essential Changes Every Leader Must Embrace* (New York: HarperCollins Leadership, 2019), 89–94.

20. Peter F. Drucker, "How to Make People Decisions," *Harvard Business Review*, July 1985, https://hbr.org/1985/07/how-to-make-people -decisions.

CHAPTER 6: INVITE THEM TO THE TABLE

1. Maxwell, *The 21 Irrefutable Laws of Leadership*, 103 (see intro, n. 4).
2. Rajeev Peshawaria, *Too Many Bosses, Too Few Leaders* (New York: Free Press, 2011), 196.
3. Bryan Walker and Sarah A. Soule, "Changing Company Culture Requires a Movement, Not a Mandate," *Harvard Business Review*, June 20, 2017, https://hbr.org/2017/06/changing-company-culture-requires-a-movement-not-a-mandate.
4. Tim Elmore, "How Great Leaders Create Engaged Culture," *Growing Leaders* (blog), November 29, 2018, https://growingleaders.com/blog/how-great-leaders-create-engaged-cultures/.
5. Mack Story, "The Law of Magnetism: You Decide When You Go and Where You Go," *You Are the Key to Success* (blog), LinkedIn, December 1, 2014, https://www.linkedin.com/pulse/20141201211027-25477363-the-law-of-magnetism-you-decide-when-you-go-and-where-you-go/.
6. See "Michelangelo Buonarroti > Quotes > Quotable Quote," Goodreads, accessed May 29, 2019, https://www.goodreads.com/quotes/1191114-the-sculpture-is-already-complete-within-the-marble-block-before.
7. Brené Brown, *Dare to Lead: Brave Work. Tough Conversations. Whole Hearts.* (New York: Random House, 2018), 4.
8. Beverly Showers, Bruce Joyce, and Barrie Bennett, "Synthesis of Research on Staff Development: Framework for Future Study and a State-of-the-Art Analysis," *Educational Leadership* 45, no. 3 (November 1987): 77–78, quoted in "Mentoring Social Purpose Business Entrepreneurs," Futurpreneur Canada, accessed January 16, 2019, https://www.futurpreneur.ca/en/resources/social-purpose-business/articles/mentoring-social-purpose-business-entrepreneurs/.
9. Syed, 11–13.

CHAPTER 7: KNOW THE GOAL

1. Caitlin OConnell, "Who Is Nelson Mandela? A Reader's Digest Exclusive Interview," *Reader's Digest*, accessed April 16, 2019, https://www.rd.com/true-stories/inspiring/who-is-nelson-mandela-a-readers-digest-exclusive-interview/.

2. John Wooden, *They Call Me Coach* (Waco, TX: Word, 1972), 184.

3. Ann Landers, "Maturity Means Many Things, Including . . ." *Chicago Tribune*, July 17, 1999, https://www.chicagotribune.com/news/ct-xpm -1999-07-17-9907170129-story.html.

4. Kevin Hall, *Aspire: Discovering Your Purpose Through the Power of Words* (New York: William Morrow, 2009), xii.

5. Luke 12:48 ASV.

6. Kremer, *George Washington Carver*, 1 (see chap. 4, n. 7).

7. David J. Schwartz, *The Magic of Thinking Big: Acquire the Secrets of Success . . . Achieve Everything You've Always Wanted* (New York: Simon and Schuster, 1987), 66.

8. Mark Miller, "Create the Target Before You Shoot the Arrow," *LeadingBlog*, LeadershipNow.com, March 13, 2017, https://www.leadershipnow.com /leadingblog/2017/03/create_the_target_before_you_s.html.

CHAPTER 8: EMPOWER NEW LEADERS

1. "Gallup Daily: U.S. Employee Engagement," Gallup, accessed March 18, 2019, https://news.gallup.com/poll/180404/gallup-daily-employee -engagement.aspx.

2. Maxwell, *The 21 Irrefutable Laws of Leadership*, 141 (see intro, n. 4).

3. Bob Burg and John David Mann, *It's Not About You: A Little Story About What Matters Most in Business* (New York: Penguin, 2011), loc. 1596 of 1735, Kindle.

4. Quoted in C. William Pollard, *The Soul of the Firm* (Grand Rapids: Zondervan, 1996), 25.

5. Quoted in Pollard, *The Soul of the Firm*, 111.

6. Ed Catmull with Amy Wallace, *Creativity, Inc.: Overcoming the Unseen Forces That Stand in the Way of True Inspiration* (New York: Random House, 2014), 173–74.

7. Ken Blanchard, *Leading at a Higher Level, Revised and Expanded Edition* (Upper Saddle River, NJ: Pearson, 2010), 64.

8. Quoted in Bertie Charles Forbes, *Forbes* 116, nos. 1–6 (1975).

9. General George S. Patton Jr., *War as I Knew It* (New York: Houghton Mifflin, 1975), 357.

10. Jim Collins, *How the Mighty Fall: And Why Some Companies Never Give In* (New York: Collins Business Essentials, 2009), loc. 791 of 4237, Kindle.

11. Quoted in Dianna Daniels Booher, *Executive's Portfolio of Model Speeches for All Occasions* (London: Prentice-Hall, 1991), 34.
12. Quoted in Manchester Literary Club, *Papers of the Manchester Literary Club* 26 (Manchester, UK: Sherratt & Hughes, 1899), 232.
13. Steve Adubato, "Great Facilitation Pays Big Dividends," *Stand and Deliver* (blog), accessed February 21, 2019, https://www.stand-deliver .com/columns/leadership/1328-great-facilitation-pays-big-dividends.html.
14. William James to Radcliffe students in Philosophy 2A, April 6, 1896, quoted in *The Oxford Dictionary of American Quotations*, selected and annotated by Hugh Rawson and Margaret Miner, 2nd ed. (New York: Oxford, 2006), 324.

CHAPTER 9: HARNESS THEIR MOTIVATION

1. Daniel Pink, *Drive: The Surprising Truth About What Motivates Us* (New York: Riverhead, 2011), loc. 110 of 3752, Kindle.
2. Pink, loc. 71.
3. Pink, loc. 174.
4. Peggy Noonan, "To-Do List: A Sentence, Not 10 Paragraphs," *Wall Street Journal*, June 26, 2009, https://www.wsj.com/articles/SB124596573543456401.
5. Gary R. Kremer, ed., *George Washington Carver: In His Own Words* (Columbia, MO: University of Missouri, 1991), 1.
6. Joseph P. Cullen, "James' Towne," *American History Illustrated*, October 1972, 33–36.
7. Pink, *Drive*, loc. 260 of 3752.
8. John C. Maxwell, *Winning with People: Discover the People Principles That Work for You Every Time* (Nashville: Thomas Nelson, 2007), 248.
9. John Wooden with Steve Jamison, *Wooden: A Lifetime of Observations and Reflections On and Off the Court* (New York: McGraw-Hill, 1997), 11.
10. J. Pincott, ed., *Excellence: How to Be the Best You Can Be by Those Who Know* (London: Marshall Cavendish Limited, 2007), 15.
11. Bill Watterson, *There's Treasure Everywhere* (Kansas City: Andrews McMeel, 1996), loc. 171 of 178, Kindle.
12. Quoted in *WJR 3* (Washington Communications, 1981), 59.
13. Stephen Guise, "Habit Killers: Four Fundamental Mistakes That Destroy Habit Growth," *Develop Good Habits: A Better Life One Habit at a Time* (blog), updated March 27, 2019, https://www.developgoodhabits.com/habit-killers/.

14. John Ruskin, "When Love and Skill Work Together, Expect a Masterpiece," *Diabetes Educator* 18, no. 5 (1992): 370–71.

CHAPTER 10: TRAIN YOUR LEADERS

1. Adapted from "The 8 Questions That Predict High-Performing Teams," *Marcus Buckingham* (blog), accessed March 25, 2019, https://www .marcusbuckingham.com/rwtb/data-fluency-series-case-study/8-questions /#iLightbox[postimages]/0.
2. Paul Arnold, "Team Building from the Ashes," *Ignition Blog*, December 29, 2010, https://slooowdown.wordpress.com/2010/12/29/team-building -from-the-ashes/.
3. Quoted in Gregory A. Myers Jr., *Maximize the Leader in You: Leadership Principles That Will Help Your Ministry and Life* (Maitland, FL: Xulon, 2011), 98.
4. Patrick Lencioni, *The Five Dysfunctions of a Team: A Leadership Fable* (San Francisco: Jossey-Bass, 2002), loc. 1914 of 2279, Kindle.
5. Gayle D. Beebe, *The Shaping of an Effective Leader: Eight Formative Principles of Leadership* (Downers Grove, IL: IVP, 2011), loc. 1029 of 3277, Kindle.
6. Mark Sanborn (@Mark_Sanborn), Twitter, September 19, 2014, 8:28 a.m., https://twitter.com/mark_sanborn/status/512986518005514240.
7. Will Kenton (reviewer), "Zero-Sum Game," Investopedia, updated May 8, 2019, https://www.investopedia.com/terms/z/zero-sumgame.asp.
8. Phil Jackson and Hugh Delehanty, quoting Rudyard Kipling, in *Eleven Rings: The Soul of Success* (New York: Penguin, 2014), 91.
9. Maxwell, *The 17 Indisputable Laws of Teamwork*, 28–29.
10. Ana Loback, "Call on Me . . . to Strengthen Team Trust," Strengthscope, accessed March 22, 2019, https://www.strengthscope.com/call-on-me-to -strengthen-team-trust/.
11. David Sturt, "How 'Difference Makers' Think—the Single Greatest Secret to Personal and Business Success," *Forbes*, June 4, 2013, https://www .forbes.com/sites/groupthink/2013/06/04/how-difference-makers-think -the-single-greatest-secret-to-personal-and-business-success/#b41cd5ee4bda.

CHAPTER 11: CHOOSE WHO TO DEVELOP

1. James Clear, "The 1 Percent Rule: Why a Few People Get Most of the Rewards," James Clear (website), accessed April 18, 2019, https://jamesclear.com/the-1-percent-rule.

2. Clear.

3. Maxwell, 1.

CHAPTER 12: MENTOR YOUR BEST LEADERS

1. "Carole King Quotes," *Best Music Quotes* (blog), July 28, 2015, https://bestmusicquotes.wordpress.com/2015/07/28/carole-king-quotes/.

2. Regi Campbell with Richard Chancy, *Mentor Like Jesus* (Nashville: B&H, 2009), 64.

3. Warren Bennis and Burt Nanus, *Leaders: The Strategies for Taking Charge* (New York: Harper & Row, 1985), 153.

4. Wooden and Yaeger, *A Game Plan for Life*, 6.

5. J. R. Miller, "October 28," in *Royal Helps for Loyal Living*, by Martha Wallace Richardson (New York: Thomas Whittaker, 1893), 308.

CHAPTER 13: TEACH YOUR LEADERS TO DEVELOP

1. Maxwell, *The 17 Indisputable Laws of Teamwork*, 161 (see chap. 7, n. 3).

2. 2 Timothy 2:2 MSG.

3. Mark Batterson, *Play the Man: Becoming the Man God Created You to Be* (Grand Rapids: Baker, 2017), loc. 817 of 2897, Kindle.

4. Mark Miller, *Leaders Made Here*, 121 (see intro, n. 6).

5. Arthur Gordon, *A Touch of Wonder: A Book to Help People Stay in Love with Life* (n.p.: Gordon Cottage Press, 2013), 6.

6. Lois J. Zachary and Lory A. Fischler, *Starting Strong: A Mentoring Fable* (San Francisco: Jossey-Bass, 2014), 149.

7. Denis Waitley, *The New Dynamics of Winning: Gain the Mind-Set of a Champion for Unlimited Success in Business and Life* (New York: William Morrow, 1993), 78.

8. Noel Tichy with Eli Cohen, *The Leadership Engine: How Winning Companies Build Leaders at Every Level* (New York: Harper Business, 1997), loc. 172 of 8297, Kindle.

9. Philip Nation, "Ministry Leaders: Do You Recruit People for the Task or Reproduce Leaders for the Mission?" *Vision Room*, accessed April 10, 2019, https://www.visionroom.com/ministry-leaders-do-you-recruit-people-for-the-task-or-reproduce-leaders-for-the-mission/.

10. Sylvia Ann Hewlett, *Forget a Mentor, Find a Sponsor: The New Way to Fast-Track Your Career* (Boston: Harvard Business Review Press, 2013), 11–12.